Eyestrain Reduction in Stereoscopy

FOCUS SERIES

Series Editor Imad Saleh

Eyestrain Reduction in Stereoscopy

Laure Leroy

WILEY

First published 2016 in Great Britain and the United States by ISTE Ltd and John Wiley & Sons, Inc.

ISTE Ltd
27-37 St George's Road
London SW19 4EU
UK

www.iste.co.uk

John Wiley & Sons, Inc.
111 River Street
Hoboken, NJ 07030
USA

www.wiley.com

Library of Congress Control Number: 2016939644

British Library Cataloguing-in-Publication Data
A CIP record for this book is available from the British Library
ISBN 978-1-84821-998-4

Contents

Acknowledgments

I would like to thank the following:

– Philippe Fuchs, who introduced me to stereoscopic science and to research in general. He was my thesis supervisor and I acknowledge my enormous debt to him. His desire to go to the limit of things and to understand everything was an example for me;

– Imad Saleh, my laboratory director, for having allowed me to write this book and for his support;

– Ghislaine Azémard, my team leader from whom I still learn many things day after day, for her kindness and continued support;

– Ari Bouaniche, who did her internship with me, for her high-quality work on intermittent stereoscopy;

– David Aura, who did his thesis with me, for his work on spatial frequencies related to perspective;

– Indira Thouvenin and Safwan Chendeb for their countless pieces of advice, their everyday support and our long discussions;

– Jean-Louis Vercher and Pascaline Neveu for all the passionate discussions on the human neurological function and visual system;

– Bruno Leroy, Claire Desbant, Anaïs Juchereaux, Xavier Pagano, Julia Philippe and Patricia Azame for their astute proofreading and their advice;

– Matthew, my partner, who has supported me for long years and sustains me day after day;

– my friends, my family and my family-in-law for having always been there for me, even in the most difficult moments.

Introduction

Devices offering stereoscopic vision are becoming more and more frequent in everyday life. We are offered films to watch with depth perception – the famous "3D Cinema" – we are offered games consoles including small three-dimensional (3D) screens, the video game industry assures us that virtual reality helmets will be all the rage tomorrow, the first smartphones with 3D screens have begun to appear, etc. Even if television screens are showing a decline in sales, 3D vision, or stereoscopic vision, is slowly becoming part of our everyday lives.

On the other hand, some professionals have already long been using stereoscopic vision for extended periods of time. For example, the review of virtual car prototypes is carried out in immersive rooms with 3D vision, some training methods are also performed in stereoscopy, scientists observe the molecules that they create immersively and in 3D, etc. For all these people, 3D vision is an important element of their professional life.

Despite this enthusiasm, more and more people report having headaches coming out of a 3D film, de-activating the 3D feature on their console or not using their stereoscopic TV screen. Some professionals reduce the use of 3D in their applications from time to time to rest their eyes. All these signs show that there are questions to answer about these techniques.

This book does not intend to explain how and why we should ban artificial stereoscopy from our lives, nor, on the contrary, to affirm that stereoscopy is not at all tiring for the eyes, and that this miracle of technology has no secondary effects. It intends to explain why it can be tiring, and to offer some paths for content creators to reduce visual fatigue among users, yet without insisting that technological advances will be able to resolve all the psychological problems linked to 3D technology.

Chapter 1 will explain the main principles of 3D vision in general and of stereoscopic vision in particular. In fact, we will see that stereoscopy cannot be studied on its own, outside the context given by all the other indicators of depth. Our visual system uses all the information at its disposal and the problems begin to appear when conflicts arise between pieces of information.

Chapter 2 discusses the elements of technology currently used to achieve artificial stereoscopy. It will allow us to familiarize ourselves with the technological terms and to be able to understand the ins and outs of each technology.

Chapter 3 will explain the known causes of visual fatigue in stereoscopy. It gives a description of the current research in this area. It is important to be able to differentiate between causes of fatigue to know which are those over which we can have some influence and which are those for which an in-depth revision of the content is necessary.

Chapter 4 quickly explains the consequences of long and sometimes uncontrolled stereoscopic viewing. Unfortunately, we do not yet have sufficient hindsight to be able to understand the long-term effects, but some short-term effects have already been measured.

Chapter 5 presents methods that might be used to measure visual fatigue, those preferred by certain researchers, those that have proved effective in certain cases and why.

Chapter 6 is a result of my doctoral work. It contains one of the two proposals which I make to reduce visual fatigue. It consists of applying blur to some parts of the image. This chapter thus explains how to do it, the algorithms used, the experiments carried out to verify the impact of this treatment as well as the results obtained.

Chapter 7 presents another proposal. It is the outcome of research that I carried out with another researcher on the subject of reducing the depth of image at the right moment to reduce visual fatigue, while allowing users to not lose the benefits of stereoscopic vision, depending on the task being carried out.

Principles of Depth and Shape Perception

1.1. Function of the eye

Before speaking about depth, it is interesting to quickly describe how the human eye and the visual system function as a whole (Figure 1.1).

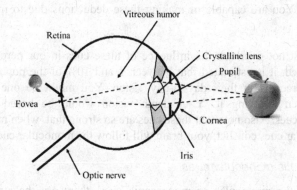

Figure 1.1. *Diagram of eye function*

When a ray of light is emitted or reflected by an object and captured by our eye, it first passes through the cornea: a transparent membrane that serves to protect the eye. It then passes through the pupil: the hole in the iris that allows the light rays to arrive on the crystalline lens. The latter is a kind of flexible lens that redirects rays of light (see section 1.2.2.2) toward the fovea through the vitreous humor, a transparent and gelatinous substance that fills the eye. On the retina, the wall at the back of the eye lined with photoreceptors, the fovea is the place with the highest concentration of these receptors. When the rays arrive at this location, they are considered to be perceived in central vision. The photoreceptors of the retina are divided into two categories: the cones, which capture colors, more numerous on the fovea; and the rods, which capture brightness, concentrated mainly on the remainder of the retina. All the photoreceptors transmit their information via the optic nerve and the optic chiasm to be processed in the parts of the brain called the lateral geniculate nucleus, the occipital cortex and the visual cortex.

1.2. Depth perception without stereoscopy

1.2.1. *Monocular cues*

Monocular cues are all those visual cues perceptible with a single eye. You do not need three-dimensional (3D) glasses to understand that, in the key scene of your favorite film, the heroes are standing in front of the background. Similarly, when you look at a photo you see immediately that such-and-such an object is closer to the lens than such-and-such a person, and vice versa. You are capable of making these deductions due to monocular depth cues.

We must not overlook the influence of these cues in our perception of depth. Indeed, it is estimated that between 3 and 10% of the population do not use stereopsis in their day-to-day vision. You might be one of them without even knowing it. Your depth vision would be based only on monocular cues. Also note that these cues are so strong that, when monocular and binocular cues conflict, your brain will follow the monocular cues.

1.2.1.1. *Static monocular cues*

Among the monocular or monoscopic cues, there are the static cues: shadows, superposition, perspective, apparent size of objects, variation of texture, etc. We use these cues when we look at a photo or a drawing or any other fixed image.

1.2.1.1.1. Light and shadows

Through its reflection on surfaces, light will influence the perception of the orientation of planes and the distance between these and the light source.

Figure 1.2. *Light and shadows completely change depth perception*

1.2.1.1.2. Interposition

When an object partially hides another, the brain interprets the hidden part of the object as being further away than the object that hides it.

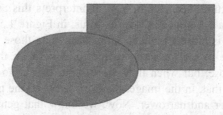

Figure 1.3. *Interposition between a rectangle and an ellipse. The brain interprets the rectangle as being behind the ellipse*

Thus, in Figure 1.3, we see an ellipse in front of a rectangle. Note that we perceive a rectangle, part of which is hidden, whereas we might have equally seen a shape with one concave edge, next to an ellipse. But it is easier to perceive a shape with symmetries than a shape with no symmetry.

1.2.1.1.3. Relative size

When objects produce a smaller retinal image when they are supposed to be of the same type, we interpret this difference as being due to the fact that the objects with a smaller retinal image are further away. Thus, in Figure 1.4, we see several flowers of different sizes, and the smallest flower will be perceived as being furthest away.

Figure 1.4. *Relative size (as well as height) gives the impression that the smallest flower is also the furthest away*

1.2.1.1.4. Variations in texture

The brain interprets regular textures more rapidly and easily, when the retinal image presents gradients of texture (in fact, gradients in the spatial frequencies of texture; see section 3.3). It interprets this as a difference in depth rather than a difference in texture. Thus, in Figure 1.5, we see that the paving stone that is closest is much more clear than those further away. In fact, it is possible to see the grain of the joins between the paving stones when they are close, but when they are distant, this is no longer possible. Similarly, we see that, in the image, the joins between the paving stones are becoming narrower and narrower. Now, we know that generally this is not the case, and we conclude from this that they are not getting narrower, but that they are getting further away.

Figure 1.5. *The further away an object, the less clear its texture*

1.2.1.1.5. Perspective

Perspective is a very well-known depth cue for all artists. There are two kinds of perspective: oblique perspective and linear perspective. The first is used in technical drawings. It does not feature a vanishing point and all edges in the depth axis are represented as parallel. Thus, in Figure 1.6, the traditional mathematical representation of a cube, we see that the edges of the cube in the depth dimension are all parallel.

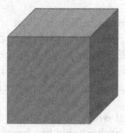

Figure 1.6. *Oblique perspective*

The second, linear perspective, features one or more vanishing points, and is that which is taught in drawing courses and that naturally appears in photography. In Figure 1.7, we see that there is a vanishing point. The straight lines along both sides of the rail line, the studs on either side, the starting points of the trees, the starting points of their leaves and their topmost points, all meet at a point located near the middle of this image. This is a very important cue for depth perception.

Figure 1.7. *Linear perspective*

1.2.1.1.6. Variation in visibility

Variation in visibility is a phenomenon that appears very far away when the weather is clear, but which can appear very nearby in conditions of intense fog. In fact, variation in visibility appears when there are particles (of water or pollution) in suspension in the air. These conceal more of an object the further away it is.

1.2.1.2. *Motion parallax*

When there is motion, as in a film or when we ourselves move, we add dynamic cues to the static cues. This is what we call motion parallax. When you move within a fixed environment, the projection of the images of the objects that surround you do not reach your retina at the same speed, depending on whether the objects in question are close or distant.

In Figure 1.8, we see that when the eye moves from position A to position B, the retinal image of the nearer apple has traversed an arc of around 180°, while by contrast, the retinal image of the more distant apple has traversed an arc of around 20°. As these two movements happen at the same time, the movement of the retinal image of the red apple happens much more quickly than the movement of the green apple. Our visual system is capable of interpreting these differences in movement of retinal images to infer which is the closer and the more distant object.

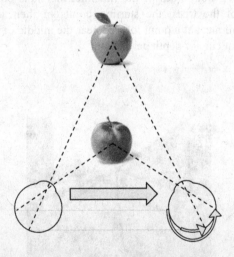

Figure 1.8. *During movement, the retinal image of a near object moves further over the retina than the retinal image of a faraway object*

Movements of retinal images are substantially the same whether we ourselves move or whether the world around us moves. This, moreover, is what creates the strange sensation when the train besides us moves: "Is it our train which is moving or the other one?". However, when our movement involves acceleration that can be felt by the inner ear, this is information which is added to the visual information. It is therefore more accurate to move around in the world than to let it move itself around us.

1.2.2. *Proprioceptive cues*

1.2.2.1. *Proprioception*

Proprioception is the sensation at every moment of where each part of our body is situated without having to look. So, we know precisely where our left hand is with regard to the right without even looking. Proprioceptive cues are information coming from the joints and muscles, which pass through the nervous system.

But what does proprioception have to do with the visual system? There are several muscles that support and act upon our eyes. These muscles come into action depending on what we are looking at.

1.2.2.2. *Accommodation*

The first muscles we will talk about are the muscles that ensure the sharpness of what we look at. Imagine a camera with a viewfinder. When you turn the bushings to move the lens, it influences the sharpness of the photo. More exactly, you move the plane of focus. The eye is somewhat the same, except that the lens does not move, but instead deforms so as to move the plane of focus (see Figure 1.9). This lens is called the crystalline lens (see section 1.1). When rays of light arrive on the crystalline lens, they are diverted and refracted as with any lens. And this change in direction depends directly on the curvature of your crystalline lens.

On the retina is that part which we call the fovea. This point is notable for having a very large number of receptors; the image captured by this part of the retina is therefore much sharper than anywhere else on the retina. The curvature of the crystalline lens will therefore change so that the image is clear on this specific area, a bit like when you move a magnifying glass so that the sunlight forms a precise point on a sheet. When the image is not sharp on the fovea, information is sent to the muscles so that they change the curvature of the crystalline lens until the image on the fovea is once again sharp. This information is recognized by the brain and it can thus deduce the depth of the fixed object.

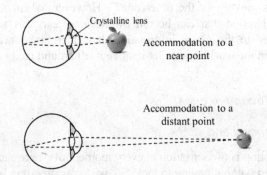

Figure 1.9. *Principle of accommodation: the curvature of the lens changes to move the point of focus*

1.2.2.3. *Convergence*

The second system of muscles to be discussed is that which allows our eyes to rotate in their sockets. Convergence is the fact that your two eyes will move so as to fix upon the same point (see Figure 1.10). When you squint, you force your convergence onto an imaginary point very close to your nose.

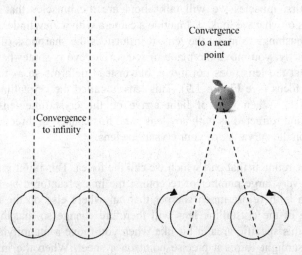

Figure 1.10. *Convergence of the two optical axes toward the point of focus*

In a normal situation, the sharp points on the left and right foveas will be the same. We are supposed to look at the same thing with each eye. If this is not the case, information is sent to the external muscles of the visual system so as to pivot the eyes until the two visual axes are pointing toward the same object. The brain recognizes the information sent to the muscles and thereby deduces the distance from the object in focus.

1.3. Depth perception through stereoscopic vision

Stereopsis is the natural phenomenon that we attempt to reproduce through stereoscopic vision. In fact, most of us use the fact that our two eyes are horizontally separated to obtain supplementary depth cues. This is what we call stereopsis.

We have seen that, when we focus on an object, the projection of its image is imprinted on your retina at the level of the fovea. This is the point on your retina that features the best acuity, the greatest number of receptors, so that we can perceive the object clearly. The rest of the scene is projected around the fovea (see Figure 1.11).

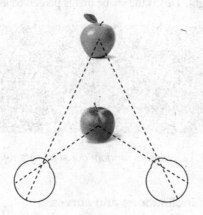

Figure 1.11. *When we focus on the green apple, the projections of the image of the red apple (which is nearer) form a more obtuse angle than the projections of the image of the green apple. For a color version of this figure, see www.iste.co.uk/leroy/stereoscopy.zip*

However, if we look at the angles made by these projections, we realize that when an object is closer to us than the object on which we are focusing, its projections on the right and left retinas will form a more obtuse angle. Conversely, if an object is further away than the object focused on, the angle formed by its projections is more acute. It is precisely these differences of angle that are interpreted by the brain to determine whether an object is nearer or further away than our focus point. The difference between these two angles is called retinal disparity.

It is interesting to note that stereoscopic cues are independent of monoscopic cues [HOW 95]. The experiments of Julesz [JUL 71] show with the help of random dot stereograms that depth can be perceived without any monocular cues (Figure 1.12). By contrast, this perception is relative and not absolute. It is more difficult to determine the exact distance away of an object without reference points than its distance in relation to another [JUL 71].

Random dot stereograms are "left and right image" pairs that separately only show, as their name suggests, random dots (see Figure 1.12). But when these pairs are presented in stereoscopy, some people do not use stereoscopic vision, but the other, when they look at Figure 1.12 with special apparatus see a square which is above the random dot. In fact, the left image is composed of truly random dots, but the right image is a copy of the first in which a shape is shifted toward the right. This is the shape that is perceived as raised.

Figure 1.12. *Julesz's random dot stereogram [JUL 71]*

1.4. Perception of inclinations and curves

1.4.1. *Perception of inclination and obliqueness*

1.4.1.1. *Analysis of binocular disparities*

Obliqueness is the rotation of a surface with respect to the vertical axis (Figure 1.13). An oblique surface creates a variation in horizontal disparities (called compression–expansion disparities or horizontal gradient of horizontal disparities [DEV 08]). As horizontal disparity is directly linked to distance, and an oblique surface shows a horizontal and progressive variation in distance, it is normal to have a horizontal gradient of horizontal disparities.

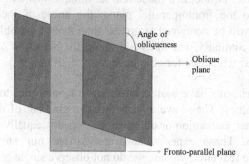

Figure 1.13. *An oblique plane produces a horizontal gradient of horizontal disparities*

The inclination of a surface, meanwhile, is its rotation with respect to a horizontal axis (Figure 1.14). As the distance of an inclined surface varies vertically across the surface, it produces a vertical gradient of horizontal disparities, also called horizontal shear.

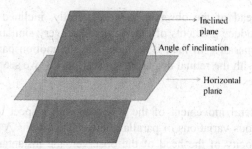

Figure 1.14. *An inclined plane produces a vertical gradient of horizontal disparities*

In a random dot stereogram, an inclined or oblique surface is perceived to be longer than two adjacent surfaces turned or inclined in the opposite directions [GIL 98]. In fact, continuous variations of disparity applicable to all stimuli are hard to perceive at a distance. A uniform gradient of disparities is more difficult to detect than a discontinuity in the gradient of disparity [MCK 93].

The perception of an inclined or oblique plane is not anisotropic [ROG 89]. This means that it will not be the same in all directions and orientations. Take an inclined plane and an oblique plane at the same angle with respect to the fronto-parallel plane; the angle of inclination of the inclined plane will be perceived as greater than that of the obliqueness of the oblique plane. Similarly, the threshold angle for detection of inclination is estimated at 1.3° while that for obliqueness is 2.1° [CAG 93].

Some experiments have been carried out in laboratories to study inclined and oblique planes. They have shown that the gradient of disparities, as a function of either inclination or obliqueness, depends equally on the distance of observation. These experiments were carried out on single planes. However, in the real environment, we do not observe single planes, but rather a great number of planes, all having different inclinations and obliquenesses. When there are several planes in an observed scene, the information is redundant and allows us to resolve ambiguities. Thus, Gilliam showed that inclinations and obliquenesses are seen more quickly and precisely when there are several planes in the scene. It is notably the presence of discontinuities of gradient between planes that improves this perception [GIL 83].

1.4.1.2. Analysis of motion parallaxes

When the head of the observer moves laterally, inclined and oblique surfaces also produce gradients of motion parallax, very similar to gradients of binocular disparities. In fact, if we compare the motion parallaxes from section 1.2.1.2 with the retinal disparities in section 1.3, we see that there are strong similarities.

During a lateral movement of the observer with respect to an oblique surface, continuous variations of parallax between positions A and B occur. For a given velocity of the head of the observer, the instantaneous rate of horizontal expansion or compression depends on the obliqueness of the surface. We call this a horizontal gradient of horizontal velocity. However, it should be noticed that a fixed oblique surface placed in front of an observer in lateral motion is not the only way to produce a horizontal gradient of horizontal velocities. A surface of different obliqueness placed eccentrically or in rotation, and a fronto-parallel surface, which is moving into the distance at the same time as the lateral movement of the observer, produces the same gradient [ALL 03].

1.4.1.3. *Analysis of textures*

"A texture corresponds to the 'design' carried by a surface (flat or curved). The structuring elements of texture possess characteristics associated with the properties of spatial distribution (frequency, randomness, irregularity, gradual variations) common to the whole region under consideration" [MAS 06].

Gibson was the first to describe a gradient of texture, which he defines as changes in the size or form of small elements of texture that appear on many surfaces in our environment [GIB 50]. These gradients of textures give us information on the distance of viewed objects (see section 1.2.1.1.4), but also on the orientation of surfaces (Figures 1.15 and 1.16), and, as we will see, on the curvature of the latter (see section 1.4.2.3).

Figure 1.15. *The gradient of the texture encourages us to perceive an inclined plane*

Figure 1.16. *The gradient of the texture encourages us to perceive an oblique plane*

Texture is an important piece of information in depth perception. However, unlike some other cues (binocular disparities, motion parallaxes, shadow, etc.), it is difficult to establish a mathematical description of it [MAS 06]. These cues appear during the projection of a 3D surface of the world (whether real or virtual) onto a two-dimensional image plane (whether screen or retina). This projection produces deformation of the textural elements.

Stevens demonstrated that the two aspects of texture (size and shape) given different elements of information concerning the orientation of the surface [STE 79]. The size of elements may be used to estimate the relative distances between the different parts of the surface in question, and thus work out the orientation of the texture of the object. This is not the case if the elements of texture have the same size. This is an example of a heuristic assumption that our brain makes in order to perceive depth. For the brain, the elements of texture that it looks at are all roughly similar in size and shape. Many optical illusions are precisely based on textures, which do not exhibit this characteristic. The projected form of the elements of texture can also indicate to us the orientation of the surface. To deduce this kind of information, the brain evidently uses the assumption mentioned above, according to which all elements of texture are similar.

1.4.2. *Perception of curves*

1.4.2.1. *Analysis of binocular disparities*

The second derivative of the disparities corresponds to the variation of the gradient of disparities, thus to a curved surface. It is also called "disparity curvature". Unlike the first derivative of disparities, the second is normally invariant with respect to the distance of observation. However, it is not totally invariant:

– it varies with respect to the eccentricity of the surface in relation to the point of view of the observer;

– the disparity curvature also varies with respect to the normal of the surface.

Sinusoidal variations in this disparity allow us to study sensitivity to disparities with respect to frequency modulation. Now, measuring discrimination thresholds for variations in disparity with respect to the frequency of this variation shows that the transfer function is a band-pass filter. In other words, there is a frequency of variation in disparity (thus, a curve), which is optimal for each eccentricity in relation to the point of view of the observer [PRI 98] (Figure 1.17).

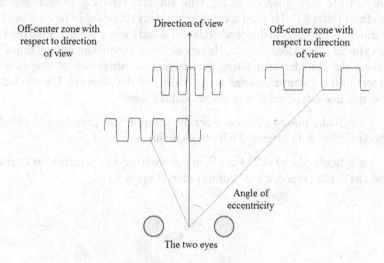

Figure 1.17. *The optimal frequency of variation of disparities depends on the eccentricity (seen from above)*

However, vertical and horizontal variations of curves are not treated in the same way by the brain. In fact, it would seem that there is a certain insensitivity to vertical variations for lower frequencies. This would highlight a certain stereoscopic anisotropy [DEV 08, BRA 99].

Rogers and Cagnello have shown that curved surfaces are more easily perceived than flat and inclined surfaces [ROG 89]. The discrimination thresholds for the orientation of curves for parabolic surfaces in random dot stereograms are very small. The authors have determined that the average threshold for curvature of detectable disparity is 0.02 min arc/deg² (for an apparatus occupying 2.66° of the visual field). However, this threshold depends on the size of the visualization apparatus in the visual field: the larger it is, the lower the threshold (and thus curves will be more easily perceived) [ROG 89]. This threshold also depends on the orientation of the parabolic cylinder. In fact, it will be 1.5 times higher for a vertically oriented cylinder.

The parabolic cylinders used up until now have been very useful in studying the discrimination of orientations of curvature. However, Johnston has suggested using circular cylinders instead, which would allow easier study of the perception of shape, with subjects referring to their internal standards [JOH 91]. He used a cylinder that was supposed to be circular, but modified its diameter in the depth axis and asked his/her subject if the base of the cylinder was indeed a circle. He repeated this experiment several times by moving the cylinder to measure the changes in perception of shapes with respect to the distance between the cylinder and the observer. He concluded from this that our perception of shapes is quite weak:

– a cylinder placed at 53 cm from the observer was perceived as circular when its depth did not exceed 67% of its radius;

– a cylinder placed at 214 cm from the observer was perceived as circular when its depth exceeded 175% of its radius (Figure 1.18).

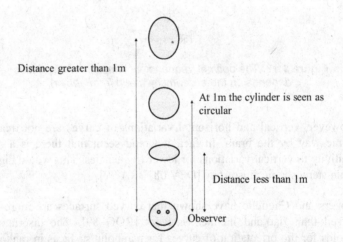

Figure 1.18. *The cylinder is seen as deformed depending on its distance from the observer (seen from above)*

He attributed this poor performance to our difficulty in establishing absolute distances in depth. As a result, the subject can only correctly assess shapes over a distance of approximately 1 m. He showed that, when the distance between the subject and the curved surface is underestimated, the curvature is itself underestimated and, conversely, when this distance is overestimated, the curvature is also overestimated [SCA 06]. In addition, this experiment took place in darkness, which made it impossible for the subjects to use other cues to get a good idea of absolute distances. In fact, Glennerster carried out substantially the same experiment with more depth cues, and the results were much better [GLE 94].

Many studies have shown that the distance between the subject and the virtual object observed was highly correlated with the way in which its shape, its size and its depth were perceived [PAL 02, PAL 04, EGG 96, HOL 41]. In fact, when the object is further away from the subject, it becomes more difficult to perceive (Figure 1.19).

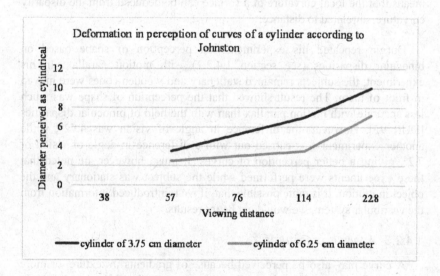

Figure 1.19. *Variation in perception of shape over distance, after the data in [JOH 91]*

Another explanation has been given for this distortion in relation to viewing distance. The screen was more or less distant from the observer to limit the accommodation/convergence conflict. This difference in screen position may have influenced the vertical disparities; these may in turn have changed the overall perception of shapes. Durgin therefore reproduced the same experiment, this time no longer projecting a cylinder onto a screen, but using real cones. The thickness of the cone ranged between 50 and 200% of its diameter, and there was a distance of 1–3 m between the cone and the subjects. This study showed no underestimation of depth in relation to the width of the cone, even when the observer was located more than 3 m from the object. By contrast, when the observers were close, there was still overestimation, but less than that found in Johnston's experiment. Durgin explained these differences, on the one hand, by the presence of other depth cues in the scene being viewed, and on the other hand, by the fact that perception of shape may be disturbed by Johnston's visualization technique [DUR 95].

1.4.2.2. *Analysis of motion parallax*

Motion parallax does not vary with respect to the viewing distance. This means that the local curvature of a surface can be deduced from the disparity curvature, unrelated to distance.

Durgin repeated his experiments on perception of shape based on binocular disparities (see section 1.4.2.1) with motion parallax. In his experiment, the subjects remained stationary and wooden cones were moved in front of them. The result showed that the perception of shape was much less accurate with motion parallax than with the help of binocular disparities [DUR 95]. However, the difference in angle of vision was 4.92°, while another experiment was carried out with a difference in angle of vision of 7.2°, giving a better perception of curves. It must, however, be noted that these experiments were performed while the subject was stationary and the object in motion. It is quite possible that, if we reintroduced information from the vestibular system, we would get better results.

1.4.2.3. *Analysis of textures*

A curve may also be perceived because of gradients in texture, or more precisely, due to variations in gradient of texture. In fact, when variations in the size and shape of elements are uniform, our brain perceives an oblique or inclined plane; by contrast, if the variation is not uniform, it will tend to perceive a curved surface rather than non-homogeneity in the elements of texture (see Figure 1.20).

Bajery and Liebermann established that variations in the frequency spectrum might be interpreted as a distortion of a homogeneous texture [BAJ 76]. In fact, when elements of the texture come closer together, due to remoteness or to change in orientation of the surface, this causes an increase in spatial frequencies (see Figure 1.21) [MAS 06].

Figure 1.20. *Certain complex surfaces can be reproduced in a realistic fashion with the help of gradients of texture*

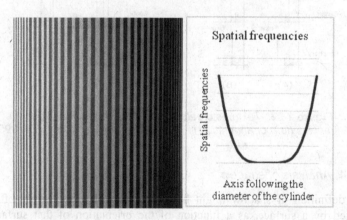

Figure 1.21. *Texture of a curved surface and the translation of its variation in the frequency domain*

Sakai and Kinkel showed that the human brain seems to follow either variations in peaks or variations in the average of spatial frequencies. Figure 1.22 shows some textures where only the peak frequencies (left) or the average frequencies (right) vary. The authors remarked that when the textures possess peak frequencies (as on the left side of the figure), it is the variations in peaks that seem to convey more information on the curvature of the surface. In the other case, it is the variations in average frequency that allow better perception of a curve [SAK 95].

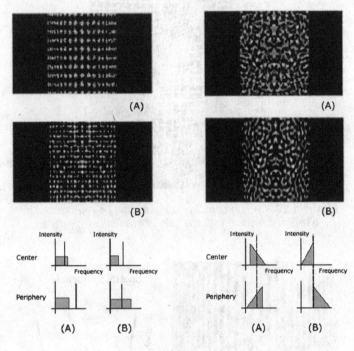

Figure 1.22. *Textures created with either a variation in peak frequencies (left) or a variation in average frequencies (right) [SAK 95]*

1.4.2.4. *Analysis of shadow*

A definition of shadow might be "a variation in the quantity of light reflected by a surface, as a function of the orientation of that surface in respect to the source of light" [PAL 99]. Shadow is a very powerful source of information. To illustrate this, consider a sphere made from a material that reflects light in a homogeneous fashion, as shown in Figure 1.23. This sphere is lit by a single point of light situated at a certain distance. We can see that the luminous intensity reflected by the sphere is not the same at all points. In fact, the point for which the normal points toward the source of light is much brighter than the point for which the normal points in the opposite direction. It is the variation of light on the surface that allows us to interpret Figure 1.23 as a sphere and not a disk.

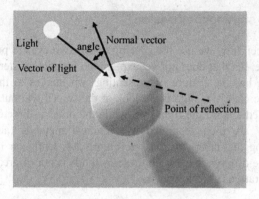

Figure 1.23. *Shadow on a sphere*

Koenderink has studied perception of the orientation of surfaces (and therefore of curves) on a human torso with regard to the shadows appearing on it [KOE 92, KOE 96]. They asked their subjects to place a gauge in the direction of the orientation perceived at certain points. The gauge is an oval with a small segment on top, which represents the normal of the surface, while the oval represents the plane tangent to the latter. Figure 1.24 represents the torso on the left and the average orientation given by one subject on the right. We deduce from this that we can perceive curves with the help of shadows and the way in which light reflects on material, without the help of binocular vision or motion parallax.

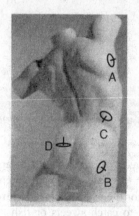 

Figure 1.24. *Orientation of the surfaces of the skin with regard to shadows [KOE 96]*

1.5. Artificial stereoscopic vision

We have seen how we use the spacing of our two eyes to perceive depth in everyday life, but that does not yet explain the function of stereoscopic 3D. This technique has the feature of presenting two images to the spectator's gaze. These are clearly visible if we look at the screen without glasses. One image is directed toward the right eye, while the other is directed toward the left eye. They are then separated by technical methods (active glasses, polarization goggles, anaglyph glasses; Figure 2.4, lenticular networks, see Chapter 2). The difference between these methods is not of great importance for the considerations to follow.

Imagine that we are watching a screen containing these two images with our glasses which only present each image to the eye for which it is intended. The axes of our eyes will therefore form an angle. If this angle is more acute than that would have been formed to look at a point on the screen, we perceive the object as being behind the screen. In this case, the image sent to our right eye is located on the right and the image sent to our left eye is located on the left (see Figure 1.25).

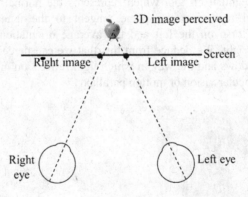

Figure 1.25. *Stereoscopic projection of an image behind the screen*

If, by contrast, the angle formed by the axes of our two eyes is larger, the image is perceived in front of the screen. In this case, the image intended for the left eye is on the right of that intended for the right eye (see Figure 1.26). Thus, it is that we can see children trying to catch sweets or fish "coming out" of the screen.

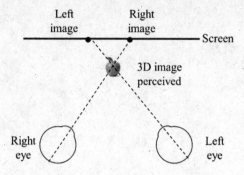

Figure 1.26. *Stereoscopic projection of an object in front of the screen*

Technological Elements

2.1. Taking a picture

A picture is taken with two still or video cameras, either real or virtual, spaced at a certain distance apart. One camera is for the image intended for the right eye, and the other camera is for the image intended for the left eye (Figure 2.1).

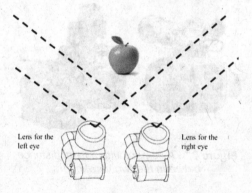

Lens for the
left eye

Lens for the
right eye

Figure 2.1. *Creating stereoscopic images requires two lenses aiming at the same scene*

If the object being imaged is microscopic, for example within the human body, the two lenses will be spaced several millimeters apart (see Figure 2.2 left). If the object being imaged is an aerial view of a wide landscape, the two lenses will instead be separated by hundreds of meters (see Figure 2.2 right).

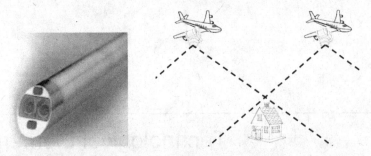

Figure 2.2. *Distances between the viewfinders may range from a few millimeters[1] to more than 100 m [ASS 06]*

If we want to obtain a perception of distance as close as possible to reality, we can choose a distance between the cameras equal to the distance between our two eyes. The average of this distance over the whole population is 6.3 cm (Figure 2.3). Professional stereoscopic cinema cameras often allow very fine adjustment of this distance.

Figure 2.3. *A camera with a fixed distance between the two viewfinders*

2.2. Reproduction

Several technologies exist to reproduce 3D images. Apart from colorimetric differentiation, there do not seem to be any great differences between them with regard to their impact on visual fatigue.

1 Use of robotics in laparoscopic urological surgery: state of the art: http://www.urofrance. org/science-et-recherche/base-bibliographique/article/html/utilisation-de-la-robotique-en-chirurgie-laparoscopique-urologique-etat-de-lart.html, accessed July 2, 2014.

2.2.1. *Colorimetric differentiation*

A decade ago, this was the best-known technology among the general public. These are the famous red–cyan glasses, known as "anaglyph glasses".

Figure 2.4. *The well-known anaglyph glasses*

A pair of stereoscopic images (left and right) are taken, often digitally encoded into "red, blue, green" (RGB). This means that each pixel bears a red value, a green value and a blue value. Our eye mixes these together to create the final color. To obtain the anaglyphic image, we direct the red component of the image toward the left eye and the blue and green components of the image toward the right eye, which are then mixed. We thus obtain a third image, which is that which we display/print (Figure 2.5).

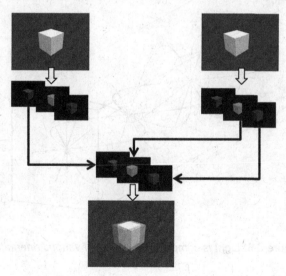

Figure 2.5. *Constructing an anaglyphic image*

The colored "lenses" of the anaglyph glasses are in fact color filters. The cyan lens filters out the red images and lets the cyan images pass, while the red lens will filter out the green and the blue and let the red pass. This means that the right eye only sees the red image (coming from the image captured for the right eye), while the left eye only sees the green and the blue (coming from the image captured for the left eye).

2.2.2. Differentiation by polarization

Light is a combination of waves of different orientations and frequencies. Frequency gives the color, while orientation gives polarization. In the previous section, we separated images on the basis of color or frequency; now, we separate them by polarization.

If we take a light wave as consisting of a single frequency (which is more convenient for representation, but the principle is the same with all colors present), there are a large number of waves which propagate in the same direction, but not necessarily with the same orientation (Figure 2.6).

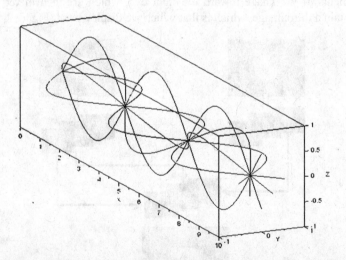

Figure 2.6. *Light is composed of waves of various orientations*

Polarization consists of suppressing one portion of these waves, so as to only preserve one particular kind of orientation.

2.2.2.1. *Linear polarization*

Linear polarization consists of suppressing all those orientations which are not that of the filter. This is done by means of tiny grids that block those waves presenting an orientation whose passage is not desired. Only waves parallel to the grid will be able to pass (Figure 2.7).

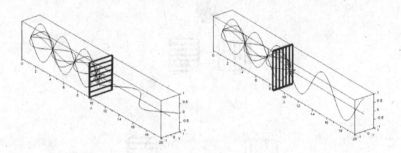

Figure 2.7. *Horizontal (left) and vertical (right) polarization*

If we place two grids in parallel, this will not change any of the luminous information emerging from the first grid, as the orientation is kept the same for both filters. In contrast, if we put two grids perpendicular to each other, the rays which pass the first grid will be stopped by the second (Figure 2.8). There are thus no more light rays after the second filter.

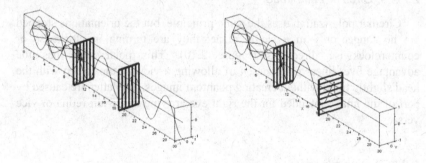

Figure 2.8. *Two identical filters will not change the initial polarization, while two opposed filters will block all waves*

If we place a horizontal filter at the output of the projector of images intended for the right eye, as well as on the lens of the spectacles in front of the right eye, the right eye will perceive the luminous information emerging from this projector. The projector for the left eye will, in turn, have a vertical filter, just like the lens in front of the left eye (Figure 2.9). Thus, the right eye will not see these images, while the left eye sees them.

Screen seen from
above

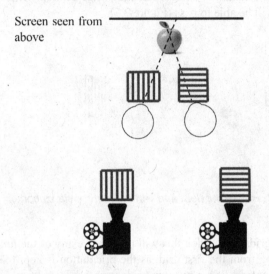

Figure 2.9. *Use of linear polarization in stereoscopy*

2.2.2.2. Circular polarization

Circular polarization uses the same principle, but the orientations stopped are no longer only in a single plane; they are turning in clockwise or counterclockwise directions (Figure 2.10). This polarization has the advantage over linear polarization of allowing a view of the screen with the head slightly tilted without creating phantom images. The latter are caused by part of the image intended for the right eye arriving at the left retina or vice versa.

2.2.3. Active glasses

This differentiation is produced by synchronization between the glasses and the screen. The screen presents the left image, then the right image, and so on. Meanwhile, the liquid crystal glasses block the right eye, then the left eye, and so on (Figure 2.11).

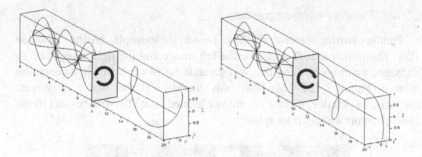

Figure 2.10. *Circular polarization*

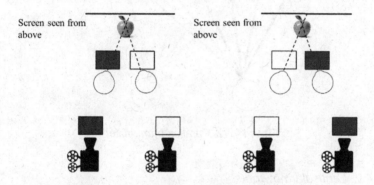

Figure 2.11. *Active glasses hide one eye, then the other, in synchronization with the projectors*

This is done too quickly for us to consciously perceive, but at no point do the two eyes see something at the same time. Either the left eye perceives its image, or the right eye perceives its own, but never at the same time; one eye is always blind. Active glasses are generally heavier than polarized glasses, particularly because of the presence of batteries.

2.2.4. *Auto-stereoscopic screens*

There are a few screens that offer artificial stereoscopy without glasses. These are auto-stereoscopic screens.

2.2.4.1. *Parallax-barrier screens*

Parallax-barrier screens are those found, for example, on the Nintendo 3DS. The principle is to interlace the left image and the right image and to introduce a compound filter that will separate the two columns in a geometric manner (Figure 2.12). This filter only functions if the user is positioned correctly. In practice, if the eyes are not located correctly with respect to the filter, phantom images may appear.

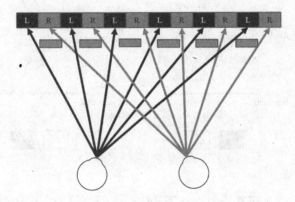

Figure 2.12. *Parallax-barrier filter*

2.2.4.2. *Lenticular networks*

Lenticular networks are composed of semi-cylindrical lenses placed in front of the interlaced left and right images.

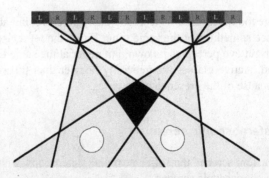

Figure 2.13. *Auto–stereoscopy by means of lenticular networks*

Each lens directs, by means of an optical effect, the column of pixels placed behind it toward the eye for which it is intended (Figure 2.13). We can see that this system is also dependent on the position of the observer.

2.2.5. *Virtual reality headsets*

A virtual reality headset comprises a separate screen for each eye. Each screen, showing left and right images, is situated in front of the corresponding eye. So that the left eye does not see the right image and vice versa, the two screens must be placed very close to the eyes. However, we have seen that the crystalline lens curves to accommodate to a certain distance; but in a virtual reality headset, the screens are located too close for us to physiologically be able to accommodate (Figure 2.14). It is necessary to place a lens between the eye and the screen to offset the accommodation. This allows us to optically place the screen several dozen centimeters from the eye, a much more comfortable distance for accommodation (Figure 2.15).

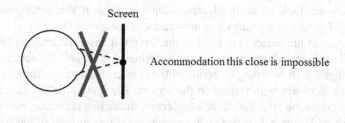

Screen

Accommodation this close is impossible

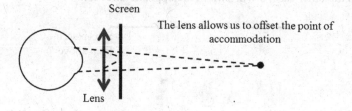

Screen

The lens allows us to offset the point of accommodation

Lens

Figure 2.14. *Offsetting the point of accommodation*

It is necessary to ensure that the lenses and the center of the screens are indeed in the axes of the eyes. Otherwise, undesirable disparities, deformations of the image and very pronounced discomfort may ensue.

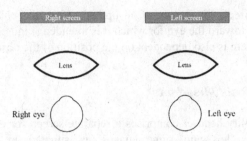

Figure 2.15. *Principle of a virtual reality headset*

2.3. Motion parallax restitution

Motion parallax can also be reproduced virtually. In fact, we saw in section 1.2.1.2 that motion parallax is an important indicator of depth.

2.3.1. *Pseudoscopic movement*

When we look at artificial stereoscopic images at the same time as moving, it produces a strange and unpleasant phenomenon: the virtual object also moves. If the object is in front of the screen, it has a tendency to follow us, while the opposite movement happens when it is behind the screen. We see in Figure 2.16 how the perception of the projected image is affected when we move sideways with respect to the screen. The images on the screen do not change, on the other hand; the intersection of the two optic axes moves. It will shift in the same direction as the movement if it is in front of the screen, and in the other case, it will shift in the opposite direction.

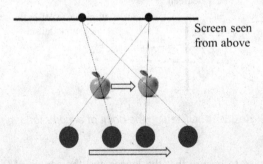

Figure 2.16. *Pseudoscopic movements caused by horizontal displacement*

The same phenomenon occurs when we move away from or closer to the screen. As we can see in Figure 2.17, if we approach the screen, the virtual world in front of the screen will have a tendency to squash together in front of the screen and to spread out behind it. In contrast, if we move away from the screen, it will spread out in front of the screen and compact itself behind the screen.

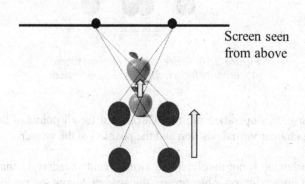

Screen seen from above

Figure 2.17. *Pseudoscopic movements caused by a displacement in distance*

We can see then that pseudoscopic movements are involuntary movements, deformations of objects and of the virtual world, produced by our own movements. We do not perceive these in the cinema because we only very rarely move in our seat, but this deformation is clearly seen in an immersive room.

2.3.2. *Correcting pseudoscopic movements*

It is possible to correct these pseudoscopic movements. To be precise, if we want the intersection of the visual axes not to move when we ourselves move, it is therefore necessary to move the image points on the screen.

We see in Figure 2.18 that, for the virtual point to be seen in the same place (in front of the screen) when the person moves to the right, it is necessary that the image points of this virtual point move toward the left. Thus, the optical axes always meet on the virtual point, which, from a perceptual point of view, has not shifted.

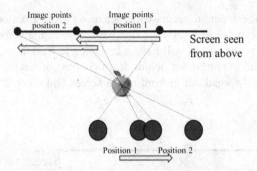

Figure 2.18. *Correction of pseudoscopic movements for a horizontal displacement*

Of course, this operation must be carried out for all points of the image, depending on their virtual position and the position of the viewer.

This technique is not involved in a virtual reality headset. In that case, in contrast to immersion on a big screen, the screens follow the person's head. On the other hand, as for immersion on a big screen, it is necessary to follow the head of the user or their point of view to be able to direct the virtual cameras toward the same position and the same orientation as the eyes of the immersed viewer.

To do this, there are several methods. I will not go into the technical detail of these tracking methods, but I find it interesting to mention them here.

2.3.2.1. *Mechanical and electromagnetic trackers*

2.3.2.1.1. Mechanical sensors

Mechanical sensors are more often used in the case of virtual reality helmets, especially accelerometers and gyroscopes. They allow us to know at any moment the acceleration and orientation of the head.

Accelerometers allow us to capture the acceleration of the device. We can deduce its position from this. However, it is still necessary to pay attention to any drift of this sensor. To obtain a position based on acceleration requires two successive integrations, which often quite quickly causes a digital explosion.

As for the gyroscope, it measures the angle, and thus allows us to easily obtain the orientation of the user's head.

2.3.2.1.2. Electromagnetic trackers

We only mention electromagnetic trackers for their historical role. We almost never encounter them any more in laboratories, but they were among the first motion sensors to be able to capture a person's location and orientation without contact. They were based on a fixed module that emitted a magnetic field and on a mobile module that measured perceived changes in that field. Based on these modifications (intensity, phase), the system deduced the position of the mobile module and its orientation. However, the system had some disadvantages. It did not work if any magnetic metals entered the area of operation. Moreover, the mobile module was quite bulky and connected to the system by a cable (see Figure 2.19).

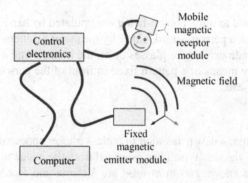

Figure 2.19. *Functioning principle of a magnetic tracker*

This kind of tracker is still sold for applications where very high-speed motion is necessary (in sports analysis, for example).

2.3.2.2. *Optical trackers*

2.3.2.2.1. Detection by conventional camera

With tag

ARToolkit is the best known system for tracking by camera with tag. It functions by recognition of a pattern arranged in advance. It was widely used in augmented-reality applications.

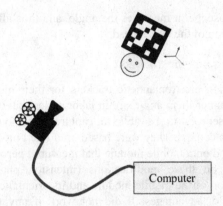

Figure 2.20. *ARtoolKit, a camera tracking system, often used in augmented-reality applications and which can be used in head tracking*

It is often used to track objects being manipulated by hand, but it can also be used to follow a person's head, either by means of a pattern attached to the head (with a headband, on the glasses or on the helmet) and a camera facing the person, or by means of a pattern fixed in front of the person and a camera attached to the head.

Without tag

Some time ago, a new generation of tagless tracker appeared. It is based on patterns that the algorithm itself has extracted from the image to be recognized. Among the best known and most used are Vuforia and faceAPI. These two products do not have the main purpose of following the head. Vuforia is more used to create augmented reality, such as the ARToolKit. faceAPI is a piece of software used primarily to recognize facial expressions. However, both can be diverted from their normal usage to carry out head tracking.

2.3.2.2.2. Infrared detection

With a target

These technologies are not very widespread among the general public, but are very much used by professionals. Infrared rays are light waves of a frequency too low to be seen by the human eye, but which can be captured by special cameras. Most require equipping the person with reflective beads. The infrared waves emitted by the device reflect off the beads and are captured by the cameras. These can be distributed around the subject, as with the conventional ART camera or Optitrack's Flex 3 (see Figure 2.21)

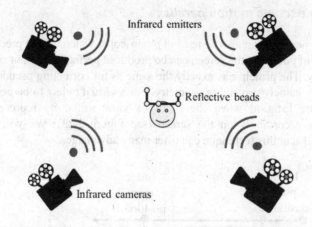

Figure 2.21. *Detecting head position by infrared with target*

Without target

Some interfaces for the general public are already widely available. Originally intended as game controllers, they can also be used for head tracking. In effect, the Kinect devices allow us to follow body movements, including the head (see Figure 2.22).

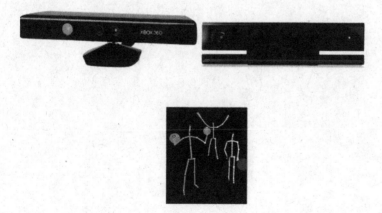

Figure 2.22. *Kinect 1 and 2 and the outlines which they capture[2]*

---

2 Kinects – Microsoft: https://www.microsoft.com/, accessed January 6, 2015.

2.3.3. *Monoscopic motion parallax*

Motion parallax can also be used in monoscopic vision. To be precise, the movement of points on the screen can be produced perfectly without artificial stereoscopy. The principle is exactly the same as for correcting pseudoscopic movements, namely projective geometry. For a virtual object to be perceived at the same location when the point of view shifts, its representation must move accordingly on the screen (see Figure 2.23). We will see in section 7.1.1 that this technique can offer many advantages.

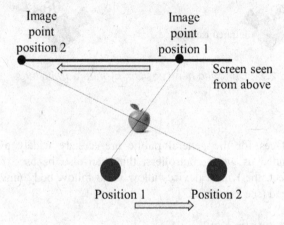

Figure 2.23. *Monoscopic motion parallax*

Causes of Visual Fatigue
in Stereoscopic Vision

Numerous causes of visual fatigue are linked to artificial stereoscopy. We will attempt in this chapter to outline the major ones and those most often cited.

In the literature, a distinction is sometimes made between visual comfort or discomfort and visual fatigue, or asthenopia. For example, Lambooij argues that visual fatigue is objectively measurable, whereas visual comfort is a subjective datum [LAM 091]. He, nevertheless, links the two in arguing that subjective comfort must be taken into account when measuring objective fatigue.

3.1. Conflict between accommodation and convergence

We saw in section 1.2.2 that accommodation (modifying the curvature of the crystalline lens to increase the sharpness of the image on the retina) and convergence (rotating the two eyes toward the point of focus) are both involved in natural depth perception. It is therefore to be expected that they are also involved in artificial stereoscopic vision. Convergence can be made on a virtual point, and therefore two eyes can converge on objects coming out of the screen or behind the screen.

However, for clear vision, we need to accommodate to the screen. If we try to adapt a lens so that an imaginary point can be perceived in focus, this will not be possible. Thus, we need to have a real image on which to focus. Now, the clear image is projected on the screen. Our crystalline lens will therefore curve itself so that the image formed on the screen is clearly projected onto the retina. Our accommodation distance is therefore the distance between us and the screen.

This is the crux of the problem: in daily life, our eyes converge and accommodate to the same point or very close to it (see Figure 3.1). In artificial vision, we accommodate to the screen and we converge on a point in depth (see Figure 3.2). If this point is located on the screen, there is no problem, but if this is not the case, if the object is perceived in front of or behind the screen, these two cues do not convey the same information. Thus, there is a conflict between them.

Natural vision

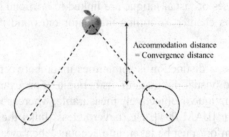

Figure 3.1. *Accommodation and convergence in natural vision*

Artificial stereoscopic vision

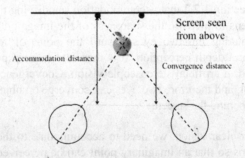

Figure 3.2. *Accommodation and convergence in artificial vision are not necessarily equivalent*

We might say: "So what? These two cues are independent". This is broadly true, but during our early adolescence, a link develops between the distances of accommodation and convergence [SCH 61, NEV 10].

Our visual system can tolerate a slight conflict, but when the conflict becomes too significant, it can no longer link the two and we get double vision (see Figure 3.3) [NEV 08, HOF 08].

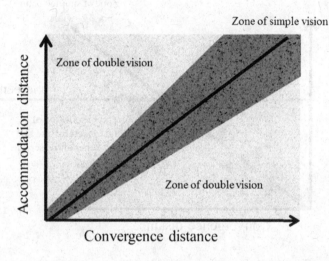

Figure 3.3. *Acceptable link between distances of accommodation and convergence*

The zone of simple vision in Figure 3.3 is useful in natural vision. This allows us to avoid seeing double when our eyes have not fully completed adjusting their accommodation or their convergence. It is a sort of margin of error. The width of this zone depends on many things. It is different for everyone, but it also varies depending on our fatigue and what we are looking at. The zone of simple vision contains a narrower zone which we call the comfort zone. According to various authors, it is parallel (Percival's comfort zone) to the line of natural vision (called Donder's line) or not (Sheard's comfort zone) [SHI 11].

When we look at stereoscopic images, as we have seen, we accommodate to the screen so that the image forms clearly on our retina. If our position is fixed, our accommodation distance will thus also be constant. If we want to remain within the zones of comfort and simple vision, the virtual object must be sufficiently close to the screen to remain in the green zone, shown in Figure 3.4. The closer a virtual object is to the border between the simple vision and double vision zones, the more tiring it will be for the visual system [YAN 02, RUS 99].

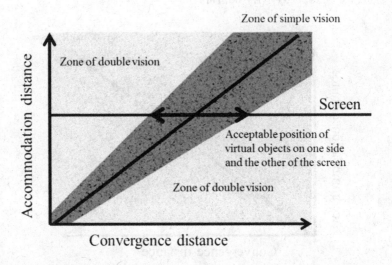

Figure 3.4. *In stereoscopic vision, our accommodation is fixed on the screen, and so we must adjust convergence so that it remains in the acceptable zone*

3.2. Too much depth

If the depth of vision is too pronounced, our visual system will tire more rapidly. This can happen without stereoscopic glasses. When we view stereoscopic images, the more the left and right images are separated, the more depth is involved and the more fatigue is caused. The angle formed in Figure 3.5 is called the horizontal disparity. It depends of course on the images projected, but also on our position. For example, if we are sitting in the front row, this angle will be much greater than if we were sitting in the back row (see Figure 3.6).

If you tend to get eye-ache or headache when watching a three-dimensional film, it is better to sit at the back of the hall. You will see the objects as being further away from you, but visual fatigue linked to disparities will be lessened. If, on the contrary, you are not prone to headaches with this kind of projection and you want to have the objects very close to you, a seat in the front row will probably be more appropriate.

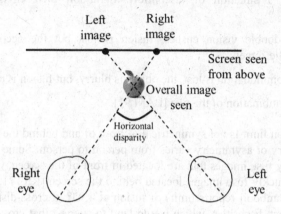

Figure 3.5. *To limit fatigue, make sure horizontal disparity is not too pronounced*

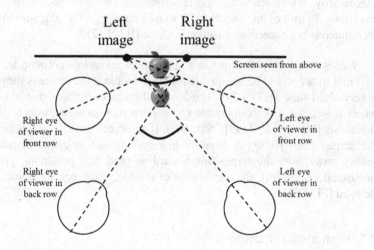

Figure 3.6. *Horizontal disparity will be much greater and thus more tiring in the front row of the cinema than in the back row*

This is a result of the disassociation of convergence and accommodation described in section 3.1. The distance of accommodation is fixed by the distance between the screen and the spectator, and so if an object displays a disparity so great that the convergence exceeds the limits of the fusion zone, this creates a situation of discomfort. Lambooij then envisages three scenarios:

– either double vision ensues, fusion is lost but the accommodation remains on the screen;

– or, accommodation is lost, the object is blurry, but fusion is preserved;

– or, a combination of the two [LAM 91].

The fusion limit is not symmetrical in front of and behind the screen, and this symmetry or asymmetry varies from person to person. Some people will more quickly fuse images that are located in front of the screen, while others will more quickly fuse images located behind the screen [RIC 71, MAN 02]. However, Lambooij reports limits of fusion at 4.93° in cross-disparities and 1.57° in direct disparities, which would tend to suggest that cross-disparities are more easily fusionable than direct disparities [LAM 91].

The literature is not unanimous on the maximum comfortable disparity (necessarily lower than fusionable disparity). Wöpkin recommends not exceeding 70 min of arc, which is 70/60 of a degree [WOP 95], while Bando recommends not exceeding 30–40 min of arc [BAN 12].

Woo seems to say that time is a factor to be taken into account; an angle of 2 min of arc would be acceptable for most people if the image is shown for a very short time [WOO 74]. The longer the object remains displayed, the easier it is to see it without double vision (although some researchers dispute this thesis [MIT 66, PAL 99]). Similarly, if an object located not too far from the screen (thus having a disparity low enough not to create discomfort) moves away from the screen and toward us (and thus presenting growing horizontal disparities), the appearance of double vision can be significantly delayed [FEN 67].

3.3. High spatial frequencies

Spatial frequency is a concept that is not often used in daily life, but which is very useful in this discussion. Spatial frequencies are a characteristic of an image, or more precisely, of a part of an image. The more quickly a picture changes, the higher the spatial frequencies. Conversely, a consistent image has very low spatial frequencies (Figure 3.7).

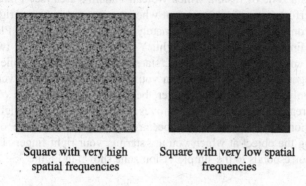

Square with very high
spatial frequencies

Square with very low spatial
frequencies

Figure 3.7. *Two filled squares with very high and very low spatial frequencies*

Spatial frequency is measured in cycles of luminance by degree. In other words, if in one degree of vision, there are three shifts and returns from light to dark, in that area there is a spatial frequency of 3 cycles per degree (3 cpd), as shown in Figure 3.8.

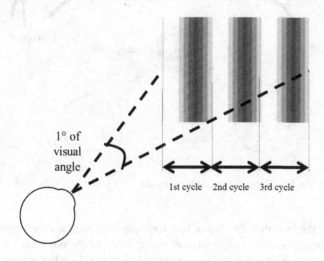

1° of
visual
angle

1st cycle   2nd cycle   3rd cycle

Figure 3.8. *Spatial frequency is the number*
of cycles of luminance per degree of vision. Here, we
have a spatial frequency of 3 cycles per degree (3 cpd)

Now, even in natural vision, high spatial frequencies do not combine very well with depth perception. In fact, around the retinal image which is formed, there exists a zone of fusion, which we call Panum's area (see Figure 3.10). We can perform a simple experiment wherever we are: put your right index finger in front of your gaze, approximately 30 cm from your eyes. Place your left index finger just next to the right. You will thus have your two index fingers 30 cm from your eyes. Next, stare at the right finger, while moving the left finger toward and away from you. If the two fingers are very close, you will only see a single left finger, because it is in the zone of fusion, Panum's area. When the left finger moves too far away from the right finger, you will normally see it double, because it has left the zone of fusion surrounding the object at which you are staring, your right finger. This zone of fusion corresponds to the simple vision zone shown in Figure 3.3.

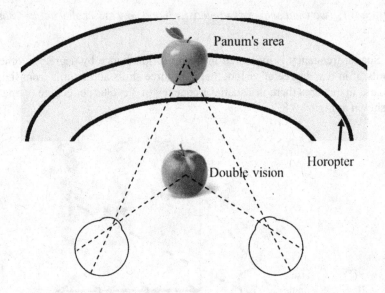

Figure 3.9. *Panum's area extends on both sides of the horopter*

The problem is that the size of this zone depends on many variables: your level of tiredness, your visual fatigue, the distance of the object in view, but also the spatial frequencies of what we are looking at. In other words, if you draw very thin lines on your index fingers and then repeat the previous experiment, the left finger will be seen double much more quickly than without lines drawn on your fingers.

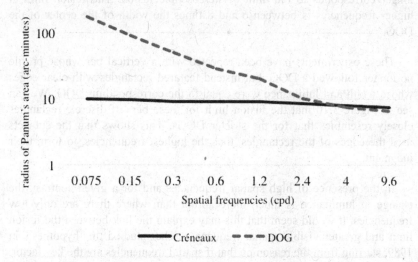

Figure 3.10. *Relationship between spatial frequencies and Panum's area, after data from [SCH 86]*

3.3.1. *Limits of fusion*

Several studies have shown that the threshold of fusion is higher when looking at an image with weak spatial frequencies [ROU 95, ROU 92]. Schor used vertical variations in luminance following a difference of Gaussians (DOG) profile. The frequency band studied extended from 0.075 to 9.6 cpd. The subjects had to adjust the two images to determine the disparity after which fusion was no longer possible. It was shown that the threshold of fusion decreased with increasing spatial frequency presented, as shown in Figure 3.10. The fusion limit in the vertical direction was lower than that in the horizontal direction [SCH 86]. When spatial frequency was lower than 1.5 cpd, the fusion limit corresponded in practice to a 90° phase shift (the limit after which the subject does not merge the corresponding bands, also called the Rayleigh limit). They thus concluded that at this frequency, stereoscopic acuity was limited only by monoscopic acuity.

For spatial frequencies greater than 2.4 cpd, the fusion limit varied between 5 and 10 arc-min. So for high frequencies, the Rayleigh limit no longer corresponds to the limit of stereoscopic fusion. The fusion limit at higher frequencies is between 6 and 8 times the width of the center of the DOG.

These experiments have been repeated with a vertical bar whose profile no longer followed a DOG, but instead featured rectangles with clear edges whose width and luminance were equal to the corresponding DOG. We can see in Figure 3.10 that the fusion limit for these bars of discrete rectangles closely resembles that for the stricter DOGs. This shows that the subjects used the edges of the rectangles, thus the highest frequencies, to form their judgment.

In the presence of high spatial frequencies and for a given contrast, the change in luminance is much more abrupt than where there are only low frequencies. It would seem that this may explain the link between the fusion limit and greater visible spatial frequency. Schor studied this hypothesis in 1989, starting from the reasoning that if spatial frequencies are the key factor, then a change in contrast or luminance would have no effect; but if the contrast and the luminance are the factors in question, then modifying them would affect the results [SCH 89]. These experiments showed that contrast and luminance have no impact in the frequency range from 0.4 to 3.2 cpd. This result was confirmed by Heckmann (working with Schor) [HEC 89]. In addition, the fusion limit was not influenced by increasing luminance or contrast while maintaining low spatial frequencies. They thus concluded that stereoscopic information is based more on spatial frequency than on luminance data. Patterson believes that fusion can occur over a disparity of 80 arc-min for a range of high spatial frequencies from 2 to 20 cpd, while for lower frequencies (0.1 cpd), fusion can occur for disparities as high as 8°.

If we suppress the highest frequencies, we can increase Panum's area. For each object not seen in Panum's area, we can suppress the high frequencies until Panum's area encompasses the object or the problematic point.

3.3.2. *Comfort and high frequencies*

Wöpking studied comfort with regard to the spatial frequencies present in a pair of stereoscopic images. He presented 12 subjects with a pair of stereoscopic images, whose content was calibrated in terms of spatial frequencies and disparities. The subjects had to focus on a real, flat object attached to the center of a screen. On the screen, images with disparities varying from 0 to 140 arc-min were displayed. The spatial frequencies of the content were controlled by adjusting the focal length of the projector; they ranged from 1 to 23 cpd. The subjects then had to evaluate their discomfort from −2 (very uncomfortable) to 2 (imperceptible) [WOP 95].

A comfort function has been established by Perrin [PER 98], interpolated from Wöpking's data. It establishes a relationship between comfort ($C(d,f)$), horizontal disparities (d) and spatial frequencies (f). In Wöpking's data, discomfort is represented by a value ranging between −2 (very uncomfortable) and 2 (imperceptible). The comfort function based on interpolation from Wöpking's data is represented below (Figure 3.11).

$$C(d, f) = a(d - d_0 - kf^{k'})$$ [3.1]

The interpolation parameters are as follows:

$a = -0.010$

$d_0 = 18.9$

$k = 221.1$

$k' = -0.74$

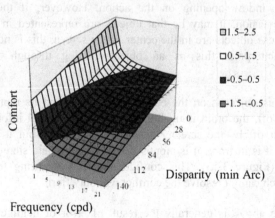

Figure 3.11. *Comfort function [PER 98]*

3.4. High temporal frequency

High temporal frequencies are slightly different to high spatial frequencies. Here, we are not concerned with a fixed image, but rather with a film or a sequence of images. The fusion zone discussed above depends in effect on the speed with which the images replace each other. We have already seen that the longer the image remains, the more chance there is for fusion to take place (see section 3.2). Now imagine that you are watching a film taking place in the Russian mountains, so involving scenery that unfolds very rapidly. If the film also presents marked changes in depth, it is very likely that you will not be able to fuse the elements in depth and that this part of the film will be very tiring for your visual system [AMN 84].

3.5. Conflicts with monoscopic cues

In our natural environment, all the monoscopic, stereoscopic and movement cues are in harmony. They all give approximately the same information. If stereoscopic vision indicates that one object is behind another, monoscopic vision will agree.

However, in artificial vision, it may happen that stereoscopic vision will indicate that one object is in front of another, while monoscopic vision will indicate the reverse. In fact, when we watch a monoscopic film, we are not shocked when the edge of the screen cuts into objects in the current scene. Our brain understands that the edges of the screen are in front of the scene, a bit like a window opening on the action. However, if the film is in stereoscopic vision, it may be that objects are represented in front of the screen. If these objects are in the center of the screen, this is not a problem; the brain interprets this as an object coming through the window (Figure 3.12).

But if this object is on the edge of the screen and its representation is thereby cut off, the brain is unable to interpret the visual information. The object is cut off by the screen, therefore it is behind; but it has negative parallax, so it is in front. It is monoscopically behind and stereoscopically it is in front (Figure 3.13). This configuration is very tiring for the visual system, which cannot resolve the conflict without effort.

The case above is generally the result of error or negligence, but if a filmmaker decides to create this kind of effect repeatedly on purpose, it is highly probable that the film will be really very difficult to watch.

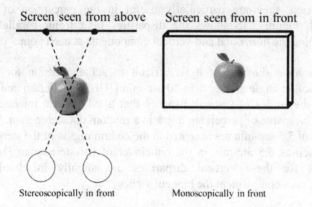

Figure 3.12. *If the object is stereoscopically located in front of the screen and if it is not cut off by an edge, there is no conflict*

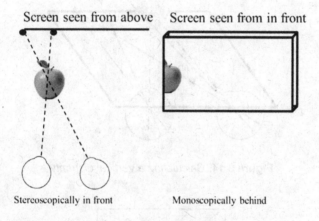

Figure 3.13. *If the object is stereoscopically located in front of the screen but cut off by an edge, then there is a conflict between cues*

3.6. Vertical disparities

The absolute vertical disparity (β) of any point in space is defined as the difference in elevation of this point between the two eyes: $\beta = \beta_G - \beta_D$ [ESP 08] (Figure 3.14). We are still dealing with both vertical and horizontal disparities, but vertical disparities are concentrated in peripheral vision. In natural vision, they are particularly useful in the perception of shapes [DEV 08]. Figure 3.15 shows the disparities in a fronto-parallel plane, distinguishing the horizontal and vertical components at each point.

Studies have shown that it is difficult to achieve fusion for vertical parallaxes of an angle greater than 20 arc-min [JUL 71]. Nielsen and Poggio measured the angles of vertical disparity that a subject can tolerate before becoming incapable of perceiving depth in a random dot stereogram. Vertical disparities of 3.5 arc-min are accepted in the central region of the stereogram, and as much as 6.5 arc-min in the remainder of the stereogram [NIE 84]. Tolerances for these vertical disparities are slightly increased when monocular cues complement the binocular cues.

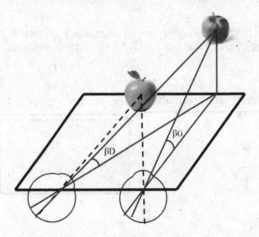

Figure 3.14. *Calculating a vertical disparity*

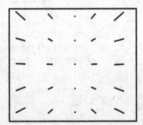

Figure 3.15. *Vectorial representation of disparities in a fronto-parallel plane*

It is thus desirable that the two optic axes of the viewpoints on the images be parallel to avoid vertical parallaxes, which will provoke discomfort with the display. Algorithms allowing the creation of synthetic stereoscopic images in this case are relatively simple and quick (calculations of translations and projections). For synthetic stereoscopic images, the viewpoints are almost always on parallel axes to avoid vertical parallaxes.

However, it is possible to have the axes of the virtual cameras converging. The positions of the two pupils and the angle of convergence must, in this case, be known with great precision. This technique allows us to reproduce vertical disparities that are more faithful to those present in natural vision. These vertical disparities contribute to better perception of distances and shapes, and increase the coherence between monocular and stereoscopic cues. This would thus reduce visual fatigue. This would be possible through tracking the subject's eyes, extremely quickly and precisely.

3.7. Improper device settings

3.7.1. *Quality of image and display*

Everything that causes eye fatigue in monoscopic vision will do the same in stereoscopic vision. The quality of the screen and projector is a key element. It is important that the cameras or imaging devices do not distort the shapes or colors of the objects. If the system is coupled with active glasses (the images are presented successively to the left and right eyes by darkening of the lenses synchronized with the alternation of left and right images on the screen), the projector(s) should be sufficiently fast to display the two images. Phantom images must be avoided; these are images intended for the right eye seen by the left eye or vice versa due to technical limitations.

When the images are projected or displayed on a screen, it is preferable to use a high refresh rate. Some people are more sensitive than others to scanning frequency, but even if the subject does not perceive it, the lower this frequency, the more quickly their visual system will tire. For monoscopic screens, a minimum of 75 Hz is often advised, even if this means reducing the resolution. This will hardly be possible with a stereoscopic screen; nevertheless, it is better to favor a high refresh rate (60 Hz).

The contrast of the display must be set correctly. In effect, the black should really be black and not dark gray. Similarly, the brightness must not be too strong; for example, a white page must not dazzle the viewer. There are images that help adjust the screen or the projector, such as that shown in Figure 3.16. In this image, the distinction between A and B, as well as that between Y and Z, must be perceptible; the color of A must be truly black.

Figure 3.16. *Image facilitating adjustment of the contrast of a screen or projector [HTT 92]*

If text is displayed and should be readable, we must ensure that the characters are large enough so as not to put stress on the visual system. Similarly, serif fonts are to be avoided. We must also avoid reflections of natural or artificial light on the screen.

3.7.2. *Differences between left and right images*

Technically, it is possible to display different images for each eye. These might differ in a number of aspects: shapes or objects presented, different orientations, different size of objects, different colors or luminosities, etc.

Let us take an extreme case: display a vertical grid for the left eye and a horizontal grid for the right eye. We perceive the two grids in superposition, but one of them will predominate over the other for a few seconds; then, the other will take over for a few more seconds. Dominance constantly fluctuates between the two images. This is what we call binocular rivalry.

Levlet [LEV 65, LEV 66] has shown evidence that this dominance changes when contrast and luminance are different for each image. He suggested that an increase in these for one of the two images decreases the length of time for which this image is suppressed by the brain. In other words, a "strong" stimulus will be suppressed for a shorter period than a weaker stimulus. An image without outlines will be suppressed indefinitely by the pattern of the other image.

This is obviously an extreme case. However, it often happens that the same image is unintentionally not displayed for the left and right eyes. A difference in overall brightness may be caused by one projector being weaker than the other, in the case of stereoscopic display by several projectors. The brain thus passes from one image to another in a more discreet, but nevertheless very tiring, manner [KOO 01]. The same applies when the colors of the two images are not identical. This is possible due to a fault in the projectors, in the projection of anaglyphic images or even due to bandwidth increasing algorithms [STE 99, STE 00]. The brain concentrates on one image, then the other, because the colors do not match.

A change in the projected height of one image with respect to the other will cause vertical disparities on the entire screen. As well as being tiring for the eyes and more difficult to achieve fusion, this also disrupts the perception of shapes. Similarly, a horizontal shift in one of the two images will change the horizontal disparities, increasing or decreasing them according to the point being viewed. If they are decreased for one point, the perception of depth and distance will change and perhaps will no longer match the monocular and/or kinetic cues. If, in contrast, the horizontal disparities are increased for another point, it will also cause changes in perception, even double vision. In fact, if disparities are increased too much, the point in question will leave Panum's area and will thus be seen double. All these situations will provoke visual fatigue. A shift in orientation of one of the projections will change the horizontal and vertical disparities of the periphery of the screen (supposing that there is no further horizontal or vertical shift). This will also cause visual fatigue.

3.7.3. *Speed of correction of pseudoscopic movements*

It is possible to avoid pseudoscopic movements while still allowing the observer to move (see section 2.3.2). However, if this technique is not correctly set up, it can also cause loss of balance or nausea [JON 01, YOU 06].

There may be poor alignment between the head being tracked and the virtual camera in the absence of movement, or a bad reaction of the latter in the presence of movement. There may also be some degree of latency between the moment when the observer's head moves and the moment when the displayed image changes to take account of this movement. This is due to the response time of the sensors, to their data transfer time to the central unit and to the calculation time to take into account the new coordinates of the observer.

When this latency is greater than 75 msec [MAC 93], it causes tension between the eyes, headache, pallor, excessive sweating, dry mouth, disorientation, vertigo, nausea, vomiting and ataxia (disorder of coordination of voluntary movement not explainable by a motor deficit) [LAV 01, MON 70]. This phenomenon has many names in various languages, but we most often use the English term "cybersickness". The theory of conflict between the vestibular and visual systems is the oldest and most widely accepted [REA 75]. The two senses send differing information to the brain, which must manage this sensory inconsistency.

One of the biggest problems with this cybersickness is that the symptoms can last for several hours after the stimulus [KEL 80], or even several days. Aircraft pilots may not fly for 24 h after having worked with a flight simulator [GOW 89].

Short- and Long-term Consequences

4.1. Short-term effects

4.1.1. *Decreasing ease of accommodation*

Ease of accommodation is the speed at which the curve of our crystalline lens changes in moving from a nearby object to a distant object or vice versa (Figure 4.1). The more tired the visual system, the more time it will take to accommodate to a point [LER 09]. This is normally imperceptible, but it can have serious consequences. Imagine that we are leaving a film and we go directly to our car. Our eyes will shift back and forth between the nearby dashboard and the distant road. If our visual system does not respond quickly enough, it will take us longer to notice cars, which might be very dangerous.

4.1.2. *Decrease in stereoscopic acuity*

Stereoscopic acuity is the accuracy with which we can perceive the difference in depth between two objects. It is expressed as an angle (Figure 4.2).

This acuity decreases sharply when the visual system is subject to the constraints which we have mentioned [LER 09]. This implies that when we leave a 3D cinema, our depth perception is lessened.

This reduction in perception will be much more pronounced for those whose stereoscopic acuity was already weak to begin with. In fact, such people put greater demands on their visual system in viewing a film, which causes more fatigue. In contrast, those with very good depth perception will become less tired and will maintain better stereoscopic acuity after the film.

Ease of accommodation
=
Speed with which accommodation
moves from the clear green apple to
the clear red apple

Figure 4.1. *Ease of accommodation. For a color version of this figure, see www.iste.co.uk/leroy/stereoscopy.zip*

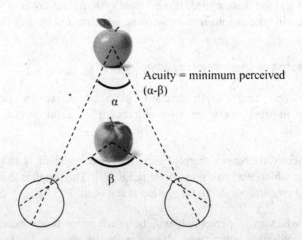

Acuity = minimum perceived
(α-β)

α

β

Figure 4.2. *Stereoscopic acuity is the minimum amount of depth perceived by a person, measured as an angle*

4.1.3. *Effects on the punctum proximum*

The punctum proximum is the shortest distance between our nose and our book, which still allows for clear vision. To measure this, we can gradually bring the book closer to our nose. We can see that past a certain distance, the words will become blurred. This distance is our punctum proximum, the lower limit of the amplitude of accommodation (Figure 4.3). The younger we are, the shorter this distance is. If we have problems with presbyopia, this distance increases greatly and we will probably wear glasses adapted to reduce it to a more convenient distance for everyday life.

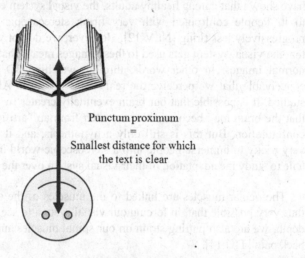

Punctum proximum
=
Smallest distance for which
the text is clear

Figure 4.3. *Punctum proximum*

This distance increases after immersion in artificial stereoscopic vision [LER 09]. Simply put, this means that we will have more difficulty reading text close-up after seeing a 3D film.

4.1.4. *More subjective effects*

Many more subjective effects have been reported. At the level of the eyes, there may be feelings of heaviness, tingling, burning, watering, redness of the eyeballs or of the eyelids. Eyelid tremors or temporary myopia may occur. Disordered, blurred or double vision can also occur.

More generally, there may be dizziness, headache and neckache. Generally, these symptoms disappear after a good nights' sleep. However, it may sometimes occur that visual fatigue accumulates over several days [ALB 02].

4.2. Long-term consequences

At present, we do not yet have enough hindsight to know what would be the long-term impact of such constraints on the visual system. Some studies have shown that among healthy adults, the visual system eventually gets used to it. People confronted with very tiring stereoscopic images find them progressively less tiring [NEV 12]. However, we do not yet know if the fact that the visual system gets used to these images means that it gets less used to normal images. In other words, through watching 3D films, it might be conceivable that we perceive the real world less well. All this is still being studied. It is possible that our brain eventually creates two "stable states", so that the brain may become able to switch from an "artificial" to a "normal" configuration. But this is still only a hypothesis, and it would be ethically very tricky to immerse people into a stereoscopic world in the hope of being able to study the adaptation of their visual system over the long term.

The ocular muscles are linked to the muscles of the spinal column. It is thus very possible that, in forcing our visual system to see images in artificial depth, we are also putting strain on our spinal muscles and this may produce back pain [TIG 14].

4.2.1. *Long-term effects on children*

The case of children is even more tricky. In effect, the visual system builds its depth perception between 6 and 12 years, and if we disturb the control loops of the visual system at the moment of their formation, this can have unforeseen consequences. From a strictly preventative point of view, it is probably a good thing that 3D televisions are not more widely sold. Indeed, if television channels had developed 3D cartoons to be watched by children for 3 hours a day and 1 meter from the screen, this could have been the source of a good deal of unsuspected damage.

5

Measuring Visual Fatigue

There are two major kinds of tests for fatigue: objective and subjective tests. Objective tests are based on optometric measurements. Subjective tests are questionnaires allowing us to determine if the person is more fatigued, if they have eye pain, etc.

Whatever test is used, it is very important to measure visual fatigue before and after immersion in stereoscopic vision in order to have an element of comparison. Both of these measurements are necessary. For example, a subject may feel some visual fatigue before beginning the test (lack of sleep, stress, long reading, etc.) and this information is crucial when we study visual fatigue after the test.

The literature is far from unanimous as to ways of measuring visual fatigue. For example, certain authors do not find any changes in the visual system after stimuli that are quite significant, although short [FOR 11, KIM 11]. On the contrary, other authors find significant changes in the visual system.

5.1. Visual acuity

Visual acuity is defined as the minimum angular separation between two lines necessary for them to be seen as separate. It corresponds to monocular performance and is also used by physicians to examine the effects and development of an eye condition [ARD 88]. We can therefore use it as a measure of visual fatigue: the greater the visual angle required, the greater the visual fatigue.

5.1.1. *Different possible measurements*

– Detection measurement: "do you see a gap in the circle?"

– Descriptive measurement: "in which direction is the gap in the circle?"

– Interpretation measurement: "which letter or figure is shown?"

– Interactive measurement: "do the letters form a word? Does that look like anything to you?"

5.1.2. *Optotypes*

An optotype is a pattern or character of well-defined shape and dimensions that is intended to check the quality of vision.

5.1.2.1. *Landolt rings*

The most widely accepted reference optotypes for laboratory use in visual examinations are also called "Landolt Cs" (Figure 5.1). They consist of a circle with a gap in it, of which the width of the stroke and the width of the gap are both one-fifth of the outside diameter. The edges of the gap must be parallel. There are no serifs. Its biggest advantage is only having a single element of difference: the direction of the gap [ARD 88].

Figure 5.1. *Landolt rings*

However, these optotypes pose several communication problems, which negatively impact their measurement of visual acuity. In fact, when several optotypes are shown in a line, there may be an error in reading direction (from right to left instead of left to right). Moreover, the subject may repeat the same optotype twice, thus causing a shift in their subsequent responses. On the other hand, as the letter C is a commonly seen shape, it is possible that those rings with the gap on the right will be more recognizable than the others.

5.1.2.2. *Numbers and letters*

These are the optotypes most commonly used by opticians and ophthalmologists. This is a test of recognizing black letters on a white background (Figure 5.2). These are ranked in lines of progressive acuity (increasing or decreasing). However, this kind of test makes it relatively difficult to control for extrinsic factors, such as memorization of the letters or the influence of the decor around the panel [NEV 08] or the emotional impact of a word (if these are used).

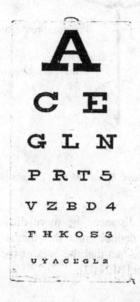

Figure 5.2. *Letter and number optotypes*

5.1.2.3. *Other kinds of optotypes encountered*

Acuity can also be measured with black and white lines [COS 96].

5.2. Proximum accommodation function

This test, also called "Donder's Push-up Test", consists of placing a visual pattern 40 cm from the eyes of the subject and bringing it closer with a speed of between 5 and 7.5 cm per second. The subject signals when they can no longer see the pattern clearly, and we then measure the distance between the pattern and the eyes of the subject. This test may be performed several times in a row to obtain an average (see Figure 5.3). Normally, it is performed with the subject using their corrective lenses, if any, first with both eyes, then the left eye and finally the right eye.

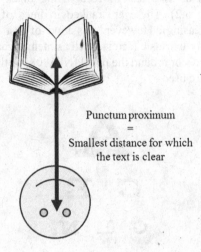

Punctum proximum
=
Smallest distance for which
the text is clear

Figure 5.3. *Punctum proximum*

The greater the final distance, the more difficulty the subject has in accommodating. We can deduce from this that a difference between two measurements is due to the fact that the eyes of the subject were more tired for the higher measurement [BEN 07].

5.3. Ease of accommodation

Also known as the "flipper lens test", this test allows us to know how much time it takes our eyes to accommodate to a new stimulus in a repetitive way. We place a visual pattern at 40 cm from the eyes of the subject and we very quickly place lenses of +2 diopters between the eyes of the subject and the pattern (in addition to the subject's corrective lenses, if necessary; Figure 5.4). As soon as the person sees the pattern clearly, they signal and we introduce lenses of −2 diopters, and so on for 30 sec.

After 30 sec, we note the number of cycles. A normal subject generally manages five cycles, and less than five cycles may signal eye strain [BEN 07].

Figure 5.4. *Flipper lens test*

5.4. Stereoscopic acuity

Stereoscopic acuity is the threshold of perception of stereoscopic parallax (Figure 5.5). It varies between individuals and the conditions of the experiment. It thus constitutes a good indicator of sensory and motor performance in the visual system, the threshold increasing quite rapidly with visual fatigue [NEV 12, LAM 91].

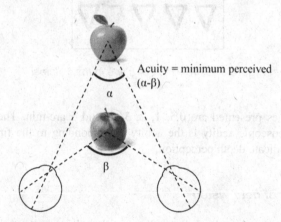

Figure 5.5. *Stereoscopic acuity is the minimum amount of depth perceived by a person, measured as an angle*

5.4.1. *Tests of distance vision*

The Zeiss Polatest [ZEI 09] consists of several polarized lines projected onto a screen. The subject is asked to determine which object is shown in front of the plane (Figures 5.6 and 5.7).

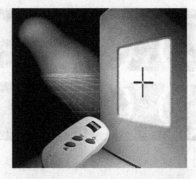

Figure 5.6. *The Zeiss Polatest [ZEI 09]*

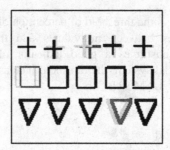

Figure 5.7. *Projection of a line in the Polatest*

The acuities presented are 0.5, 1, 2, 3, 4, and 5 arc-min. The subject's distance stereoscopic acuity is the acuity corresponding to the first line for which they indicate depth perception.

5.4.2. *Tests of near vision*

When carrying out the following tests, the visual patterns are placed 40 cm from the eyes of the subject, perpendicular to the axis of vision. They must be illuminated by means of a sufficiently powerful, normal light source.

5.4.2.1. *Fly test*

The "fly test" represents, as its name suggests, a fly in three dimensions seen from above (Figure 5.8). The wings are beneath the plane (2 or 3 cm) and the subject must try to catch them with their fingers. We note the height perceived by the subject as well as their speed of execution.

Figure 5.8. *Fly test*

5.4.2.2. *Wirt test*

This is a polarized photo of a point among a set of four points and in a series of nine figures (Figure 5.9). The subject must indicate which point is raised compared to the others. Acuities measured may vary from 800 arc-sec for test no. 1 (the disparity is such that we can see in Figure 5.9 that for test no. 1, it is the lower disc that is highlighted) to 40 arc-sec for test no. 9.

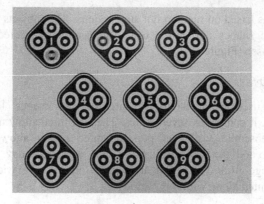

Figure 5.9. *Wirt points*

5.4.2.3. *Lang test*

This test, developed by Professor Lang, is not actually used to measure precise stereoscopic acuity, but more to determine if a person possesses stereoscopic vision. It is based on random dot stereograms representing shapes with stereoscopic acuity. Children must work out what shape they perceive (car, elephant) (Figure 5.10).

Figure 5.10. *Lang test [MC2 16]*

5.4.2.4. *Randot test*

This test is based on random dot stereograms. The subjects must identify six geometric shapes during the test. The acuities presented range from 400 to 20 arc-sec (Figure 5.11).

5.4.2.5. *TNO test*

This test uses anaglyphs to separate the two images, left and right (Figure 5.12). It comprises seven plates. The first three allow us to establish if near stereoscopic vision is present, three others allow quantitative measurement, and the last highlights a lack of stereoscopy. The acuities measured range from 15 to 480 arc-sec. It thus has the widest range of acuities presented along with the Wirt test.

Figure 5.11. *Randot test [PRE 09]*

Figure 5.12. *TNO test [MC2 16]*

5.5. Disassociated heterophorias

Heterophoria is a deviation of the visual axes, kept latent by the fusion reflex [HUG 65] (Figure 5.13). Heterophoria can therefore only be demonstrated when the tendency to fusion is briefly suppressed. It is therefore necessary to place the ocular pair in a passive position, preventing fusion. If there is no deviation before the experiment and marked deviation afterward, we can therefore deduce some adaptation.

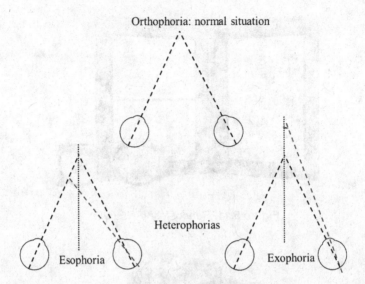

Figure 5.13. *Different heterophorias*

The only objective way to demonstrate a modification of phoria is to cover one eye. When this cover is removed, the vergence of the eye will be seen. However, this method is not susceptible to simple measurement. In all the other tests, the subject is asked to describe what they see. These are therefore subjective methods. However, this test will reveal more an adaptation to a forced phoria than visual fatigue.

Shibata has shown a strong correlation between heterophorias and visual discomfort [SHI 11]. In contrast, Karpica and Howart show only an insignificant correlation between the two data [KAR 13].

5.6. Fusional reserves

Fusional reserves are the extreme conditions at which we can fuse a stereoscopic stimulus.

It consists of presenting two images with a disparity not normally fusionable, and bringing them closer until the subject achieves fusion (Figure 5.14). The disparity at which the subject achieves fusion is called the point of fusion. The point of rupture is found by the opposite process: a stimulus with zero disparity is presented, and the disparity is progressively increased until the subject can no longer achieve fusion (Figure 5.15).

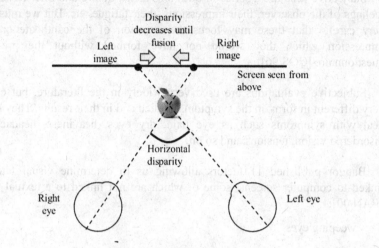

Figure 5.14. *Point of fusion*

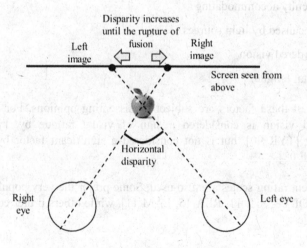

Figure 5.15. *Point of rupture of fusion*

The points of rupture and fusion are not identical and are good indicators of stereoscopic visual fatigue.

5.7. Subjective tests

Subjective tests are a series of questions asked before and after tests: the feelings of the observer, their impressions, their fatigue, etc. But we must be very careful that these may focus the attention of the candidate on an impression which they would not have formed without the pre-test questionnaire [COS 96].

Subjective evaluations are used very widely in the literature, but often very different in form, in the symptoms studied and in their results. They may deal with symptoms such as eye pain, dry eyes, heaviness, headaches, disordered vision, tensions, and so on.

Bangor published 11 factors allowing us to determine visual fatigue linked to computer screens, some of which are not linked to a textual task [BAN 00]:

– weeping eyes

– irritated eyes

– burning eyes

– difficulty accommodating

– pain caused by light sources

– disordered vision

– mental fatigue.

Some of these factors are subject to dissenting opinions. For example, disordered vision is considered a sign of visual fatigue by Tyrell and Leibowitz [TYR 90], but is not considered a significant factor by Sheedy et al. [SHE 03].

Different rating scales are also used. Some prefer the very popular Likert scales [HOF 08, SHI 11, REA 15, LAM 11], while others prefer continuous rating scales.

Reducing Spatial Frequencies

6.1. Principle

We saw in section 3.3 that high spatial frequencies can induce discomfort in stereoscopy. Perrin [PER 98] proposed a technique suppressing high spatial frequencies in areas of large disparities, demonstrating a subjective improvement in visual comfort. The idea is to extend this experiment to an immersive situation with motion parallax, thus using an algorithm that operates in real time (60 frames/sec). In addition, Perrin measured comfort based on subjective questions. We therefore wanted to perform measurements of the state of the visual system before and after immersion, so as to have more precise indicators of comfort or visual fatigue. Suppressing high spatial frequencies relaxes the accommodation. If we direct this relaxation of accommodation to the areas of highest disparity, that is areas of the most marked conflict between vergence and accommodation, we can succeed in reducing this conflict by imposing a less strict accommodation, which will then more easily follow the stimulus of convergence [FUJ 14].

6.2. Technical solution

We envisaged three computer-based techniques to accomplish this reduction in spatialized spatial frequencies. All of the following algorithms were carried out on grayscale images. Images used in practice will be in color, but the treatments will be carried out based on luminance, which corresponds to grayscale levels, to avoid performing the same treatment two more times. For all these algorithms, one important constraint is that the calculations must be performed in "real time" for our virtual reality applications (in practice, the stereoscopic pairs of images must be processed within 40 msec, if possible).

6.2.1. *Wavelets*

6.2.1.1. *Introduction to wavelets*

Fourier transforms are well known in the scientific community. They allow us to identify the frequencies present in a periodic time signal or an image. But as useful as this tool is, it does not allow us to localize these frequencies. It is true that calculating the frequency at a point has no physical meaning. However, we want to know the locations of the high frequencies in our images, since these are the frequencies that pose a problem when they are in the same location as high disparities.

The wavelet transform passes the signal through a series of filters, so as to extract the frequencies present and in particular the places where they occur. For a signal in two dimensions (data, time), we obtain either a three-dimensional graph (frequency, value, time) or a succession of two-dimensional graphs (value, time), which indicate the presence of a given frequency at a given time.

6.2.1.1.1. Fourier transform

Definition of a Fourier transform

DEFINITION 6.1. (Fourier transform).– *The Fourier transform F links spacetime with a dual space in which ω represents frequency. All temporal signals f can be linked with a Fourier transform* $\hat{\omega}$:

$$\forall f \in l^2(\Re), \hat{f}(\omega) = F[f](\omega) = \frac{1}{\sqrt{2\pi}} \int\limits_{-\infty}^{+\infty} f(t)e^{-j\omega t} dt \qquad [6.1]$$

Its inverse transform is written as:

$$f(t) = F^{-1}[\hat{f}](t) = \frac{1}{\sqrt{2\pi}} \int\limits_{-\infty}^{+\infty} \hat{f}(\omega)e^{-j\omega t} d\omega \qquad [6.2]$$

Properties

The transform conserves the scalar product:

$$\int f(t)\overline{g}(t)dt = \int \hat{f}(\omega)\overline{\hat{g}(\omega)}d\omega \qquad [6.3]$$

It conserves energy (Parseval's identity):

$$\int |f(t)|^2 \, dt = \int |\hat{f}(\omega)|^2 \, d\omega \qquad [6.4]$$

There are also properties of expansion and translation:

$$f(t-b)\longrightarrow e^{jb\omega}\hat{f}(\omega)$$

$$f(at)\longrightarrow \frac{1}{a}\hat{f}(\frac{\omega}{a}) \qquad [6.5]$$

$$f(-t)\longrightarrow \overline{\hat{f}(\omega)}$$

$$f'(t)\longrightarrow j\omega\hat{f}(\omega)$$

Before stating the following property, let us remember the definition of a convolution.

DEFINITION 6.2.– *The convolution r of two functions s and k is defined by*:

$$r(t) = (s*k)(t) = \int s(\tau)k(t-\tau)d\tau \qquad [6.6]$$

*where * denotes the convolution operator.*

The product of temporal space is transformed into the convolution in frequential space and vice versa:

$$F[s*k] = F[s]F[k]$$

and

$$F[sk] = F[s]*F[k] \qquad [6.7]$$

6.2.1.1.2. Fast Fourier transform

The fast Fourier transform (FFT) is applied to digital signals and speeds up calculation for the normal Fourier transform. In effect, for a signal of n samples, n^2 operations are required to obtain the Fourier transform by the normal method. In contrast, with the FFT, we end up with n.log(n) operations [GRE 03].

We start with a sample s that contains n values of u, where n is a power of 2. We first sort the values according to their position – even or odd – into two vectors, and then repeat the same operation with these two vectors until there is no more than one item in each group (Figure 6.1).

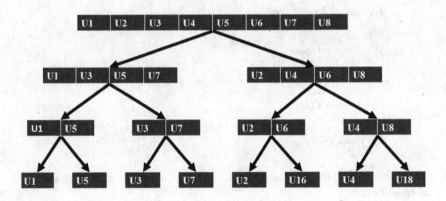

Figure 6.1. *Even–odd decomposition*

When we have this sequence of numbers, we add the elements together in pairs, after having multiplied the odd element by $e^{2ki/\pi}$, where k is its intended order in the subsequent vector (Figure 6.2).

The vector thus obtained is the Fourier transform of vector s. For the inverse transform, we use exactly the same algorithm, except that when we obtain the final vector, we must take its conjugate to get the result of the inverse transform.

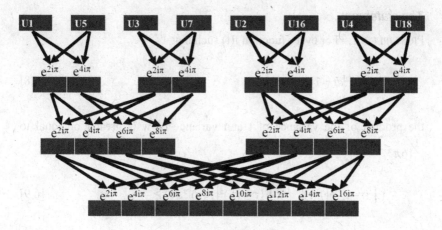

Figure 6.2. *End of the FFT*

6.2.1.1.3. Interpretation

We have seen that the transform is bijective. There is exactly the same information in the function as in its transform, since we can as easily construct one from the other. But the way we express them and their interpretations are different. In temporal space, it is possible to know the shape and the amplitude of the signal, but the frequencies present therein are not directly readable. In contrast, in frequential space, it is the opposite; we know the frequencies present in the signal without exactly knowing their shape, or the temporal location of these frequencies. To obtain these two pieces of information, we must move to a time–frequency representation as in a sliding Fourier transform, or a timerank as in a wavelet transform.

6.2.1.1.4. Sliding window Fourier transform

To fill this gap, Gabor [GAB 46] proposed limiting the Fourier transform to a "window" and shifting the window along the signal. This allows us to determine the frequencies present in a certain time period.

Heisenberg's uncertainty principle

We cannot describe a signal as precisely as we would like in both frequency and time simultaneously. It is not possible to have a very small Fourier window and to be able to discover all the frequencies therein.

The statement

PRINCIPLE 6.1.– For every function f(t) such that

$$\int_{-\infty}^{+\infty} |f(t)^2|dt = 1 \qquad [6.8]$$

the product of the variance of t and variance of w is greater or equal to $\frac{1}{16\pi^2}$:

$$(\int_{-\infty}^{+\infty} (t-t_m)^2 |f(t)|^2 dt)(\int_{-\infty}^{+\infty} (\tau-\tau_m)^2 |\hat{f}(\tau)|^2 d\tau) \geq \frac{1}{16\pi^2} \qquad [6.9]$$

6.2.1.1.5. Time–frequency representations

If we want to precisely determine the time, we must be content with less precise frequencies and vice versa. We can represent this constraint on the time–frequency plane. This plane is divided into rectangles of area $\Delta t \Delta \omega$, and the uncertainty principle tells us that the maximum area of these rectangles is $1/4\pi$. However, depending on the base used, these rectangles will be oriented differently in the plane [HUB 95] (Figure 6.3).

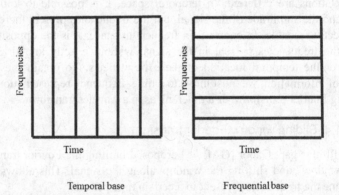

Figure 6.3. *Time–frequency plane on both temporal and Fourier bases*

In the sliding window Fourier transform, we have a sort of compromise. We separate the plane into rectangles of equal area, but whose precision in time is equal to that of the sliding window, which creates a grid pattern on the plane (Figure 6.4).

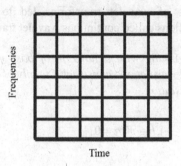

Time

Sliding window Fourier
transform

Figure 6.4. *Time–frequency plane for sliding window Fourier transform*

The most effective way would be to perform a progressive grid division (Figure 6.5). Using a large window for low frequencies and a very small window for very high frequencies would seem appropriate.

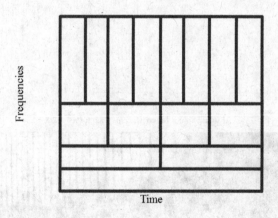

Time

Wavelet transform

Figure 6.5. *Time–frequency plane for wavelets*

6.2.1.2. *Wavelet transform*

6.2.1.2.1. Definition of wavelet transform

The first theories of wavelet transforms led to the elaboration of continuous representations called continuous wavelet transforms [RAN 01].

DEFINITION 6.3.– *Beginning with a function of base* ψ, *called the mother wavelet or analys and wavelet, we construct a family of elementary functions by expansion and translation:*

$$\psi_{a,b} = \frac{1}{\sqrt{a}}\psi(\frac{t-b}{a}), b \in \Re, a \neq 0 \qquad\qquad [6.10]$$

The signal coefficients are therefore the numbers:

$$O[f](a,b) = \langle f, \psi_{a,b} \rangle = \int_{-\infty}^{+\infty} f(t)\overline{\psi_{a,b}(t)}dt \qquad\qquad [6.11]$$

Take, for example, the function f(x)=cos(x/100)². Its decomposition is shown in Figure 6.6.

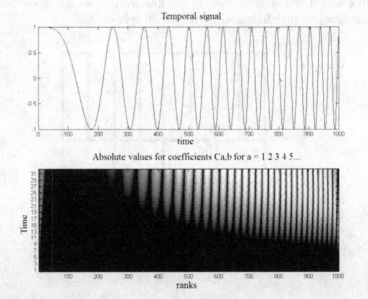

Figure 6.6. *Decomposition of a 1D signal into continuous wavelets*

We see that the higher the frequencies in the temporal signal, the more the high frequencies are shown as bright (and therefore elevated) in the wavelet signal. We also see that the more precise the time, the less precise the frequencies. This is particularly apparent when the frequencies are very high. The time is very precise, but the high frequencies are spread out over almost the whole range. We can reconstruct the original function.

DEFINITION 6.4.– *If the function* $\psi \in L^1 \cap L^2$

$$\int \frac{|\hat{\psi}(\omega)|^2}{|\omega|} = K \prec +\infty \text{, with } \hat{\psi} = F[\psi] \qquad [6.12]$$

$$\|\psi\|_2 = 1 \qquad [6.13]$$

Then, the signal can be reconstructed from its coefficients by the formula:

$$f(t) = \frac{1}{K} \iint_{\Re_2} O[f](a,b)\psi_{a,b}(t)\frac{dadb}{a^2} \qquad [6.14]$$

Note the conservation of energy is given as:

$$\frac{1}{K} = \iint_{\Re_2} |O[f](a,b)|^2 \frac{dadb}{a^2} = \int_{-\infty}^{+\infty} |f(t)|^2 dt \qquad [6.15]$$

6.2.1.2.2. Two-dimensional wavelet transform

In two-dimensional wavelet transform, the definition equation of the previous section becomes:

$$\psi_{a,b,R_\vartheta}(x) = \frac{1}{a}\psi(R_\vartheta \frac{x-b}{a}), b \in \Re, a \neq 0 \qquad [6.16]$$

We obtain the following graphic results. The original drawing is shown in Figure 6.7, whereas the first decomposition is shown in Figure 6.8.

6.2.1.2.3. Mallat algorithm

The Mallat algorithm, also known as fast wavelet transform, is that used in most decompositions of images [MAL 00, MEY 92]. It consists of passing the discrete signals through low-pass and high-pass filters recursively.

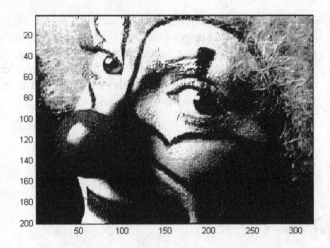

Figure 6.7. *Figure to be decomposed*

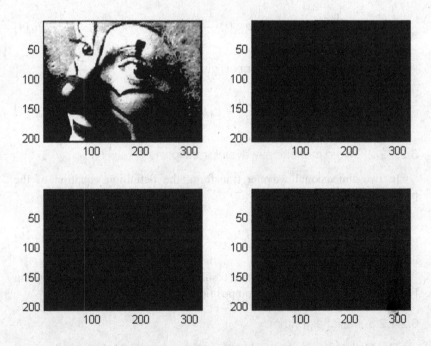

Figure 6.8. *Wavelet decomposition of an image*

6.2.1.2.4. Fast wavelet transform in 1 dimension

The original signal is simultaneously processed by a high-pass filter and its associated low-pass filter, followed by a sampling, as illustrated in Figure 6.9. We apply the illustrated recursion in Figure 6.10. The signal emerging from the low-pass filter re-enters the following system of filters.

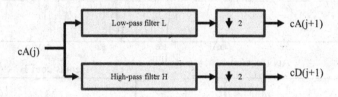

Figure 6.9. *Decomposition of a 1D signal by a Mallat algorithm*

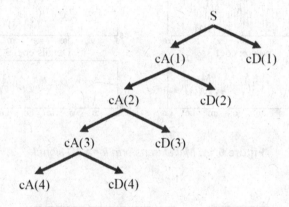

Figure 6.10. *The Mallat algorithm pyramid*

Returning to the example of the function $f(x) = \cos(x/100)^2$, this gives the transform shown in Figure 6.11.

Note in passing that every time the size of the signal is divided by two. Now the signal must be recomposed. To do this, we start from the last recomposition, in which we interpose zeros among the data. We do the same with the high-frequency data, then we pass the two vectors resulting from this operation through associated high-pass and low-pass reconstruction filters. Then, we add the two vectors emerging from these filters. This part of the algorithm is specified in Figure 6.12.

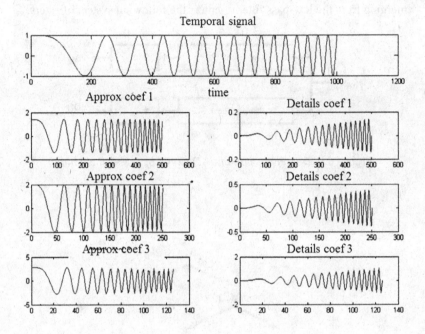

Figure 6.11. *Mallat transform for a 1D signal*

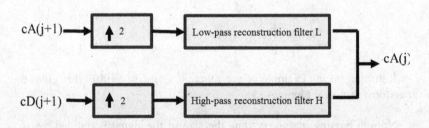

Figure 6.12. *Malla reconstruction algorithm for one dimension*

It remains to calculate the reconstruction filters based on the decomposition filters. If we name h_0 the low-pass filter and h_1 the high-pass filter of decomposition, we name g_0 the low-pass filter and g_1 the high-pass filter of recomposition:

$$g_0[n] = \alpha^{-1}(-1)^n h_1[n] \qquad\qquad\qquad [6.17]$$

and

$$g_1[n] = \alpha^{-1}(-1)^n h_0[n] \qquad\qquad\qquad [6.18]$$

with

$$\alpha = \frac{1}{2}(h_0^{dc} h_1^{nyq} + h_1^{dc} h_0^{nyq}) \qquad\qquad\qquad [6.19]$$

where h_b^{dc} corresponds to the filter gain for the analysis phase at the DC frequency and h_b^{nyq} corresponds to the filter gain for the analysis phase at the Nyquist frequency.

$$h_b^{dc} = \sum_n h_b[n]$$

$$h_b^{nyq} = \sum_n (-1)^n h_b[n] \qquad\qquad\qquad [6.20]$$

for $b = 0, 1$.

6.2.1.2.5. Fast wavelet transformation in two dimensions

The two-dimensional algorithm is not very different from the one-dimensional algorithm. It simply means applying it twice in a row, once for the rows, again for the columns. We take the data in rows to which we apply the Mallat algorithm for one dimension. This creates two images whose width is half that of the original image but whose height has not changed. The columns of these latter pass in turn through the same filtering system. We thus have four images, whose height and width are half the size as those of the original image. This part of the algorithm is illustrated in Figure 6.13.

Recomposition is also not very different. We must take care to recompose the two intermediary images. To do this, we use the columns of the four final images, and we pass these through the reconstruction filter system of the one-dimensional Mallat algorithm. We recreate our two images whose width is less than their height. Then, we take the lines of these two images to reconstruct our original image via the reconstruction filter system. This part of the algorithm is illustrated in Figure 6.14.

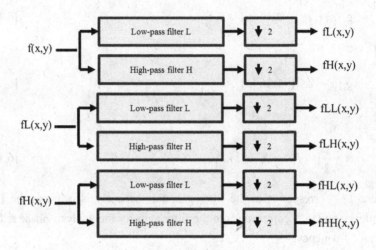

Figure 6.13. *Wavelet decomposition of an image*

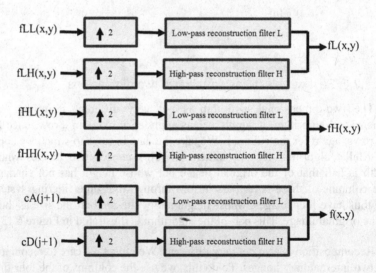

Figure 6.14. *Fast wavelet transformation of an image*

6.2.1.3. *Fast Fourier transform or convolution*

When a signal passes through a filter, a convolution is performed between the filter and the signal. However, we saw in section 6.2.1.1 that the convolution of two signals equals the product of their Fourier transform. Thus, we might wonder if it is not preferable to carry out these operations with the FFTs rather than calculating the convolution each time. Given that, this operation uses the most calculation time. To determine which way of proceeding would be the quickest, we make a calculation of complexity for a square image of edge length n. The complexity of a FFT for one line is:

$$n \log(n) \tag{6.21}$$

Since we need both a FFT and an inverse FFT, we arrive at:

$$2.n \log(n) \tag{6.22}$$

We must perform the multiplication with the filter's FFT, and the result for one row is given as:

$$2.n \log(n) + n \tag{6.23}$$

Since we must deal with all the rows:

$$n(2.n \log(n) + n) = 2n^2 \log(n) + n^2 \tag{6.24}$$

and all the columns:

$$4n^2 \log(n) + 2n^2 \tag{6.25}$$

Compare this with the convolution: for one row, each element is multiplied by all the elements of the filter:

$$n.n_{filter} \tag{6.26}$$

where n_{filter} is the number of samples necessary to describe the filter.

Multiplied by the number of rows:

$$n^2.n_{filter} \tag{6.27}$$

Then, all the columns:

$$2n^2.n_{filter} \hspace{10cm} [6.28]$$

Compare the two curves in Figure 6.15. We see that the number of operations involved in using the convolution depends very much on the length of the filter, and thus on the kind of wavelets used. When we use the FFT, on the contrary, the number of operations does not depend on the wavelet used. We therefore see that for a certain length of filter, the use of the convolution will no longer be worthwhile from the point of view of the number of operations carried out, but for the Haar and Daubechies wavelets, it will be better to use the convolution than the FFT.

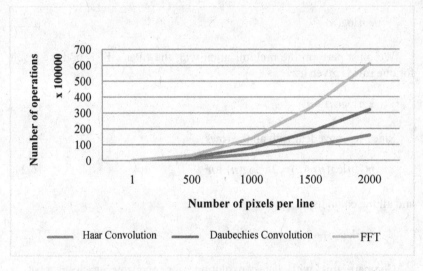

Figure 6.15. *Theoretical comparison between the number of operations for a FTT product and for a convolution. For a color version of this figure, see www.iste.co.uk/leroy/stereoscopy.zip*

The Mallat algorithm has been implemented in C++ using both the FFT and the convolution to carry out speed testing. The convolution is much faster than its rival. The following figures give the time for one, two, three and four decompositions and recompositions with the Haar wavelet (Figures 6.17 and 6.18).

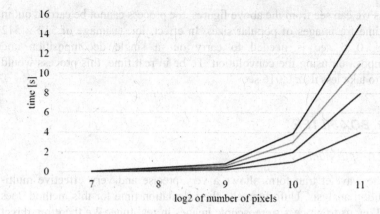

-1 decompositions and recompositions -2 decompositions and recompositions
-3 decompositions and recompositions -3 decompositions and recompositions

Figure 6.16. *Decomposition and recomposition time
for the convolution. For a color version of this figure, see
www.iste.co.uk/leroy/stereoscopy.zip*

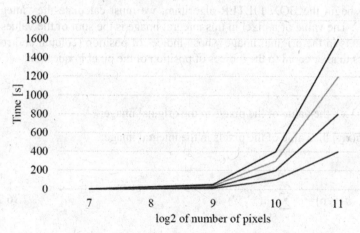

-1 decompositions and recompositions -2 decompositions and recompositions
-3 decompositions and recompositions -4 decompositions and recompositions

Figure 6.17. *Decomposition and recomposition time with
the Fourier transform. For a color version of this
figure, see www.iste.co.uk/leroy/stereoscopy.zip*

As we can see from the above figures, the process cannot be carried out in real time for images of popular sizes. In effect, for an image of 512 × 512 pixels, 0.25 sec is needed to carry out a single decomposition and recomposition using the convolution. To be in real time, this process would need to take less than 0.016 sec.

6.2.2. *BOX FILTER*

6.2.2.1. *Introduction*

The wavelet transform allows a very precise and very effective multi-resolution analysis. Unfortunately, the calculation time for this method does not allow us to process stereoscopic images in real time. We therefore direct our attention to other faster multi-resolution analysis methods, without prejudice to the general effectiveness of the algorithm. The BOX FILTER algorithm allows this multi-resolution analysis [VIO 01]. It is used to identify points of interest, but it can be slightly altered to detect high frequencies.

6.2.2.2. *Integral image*

To begin the BOX FILTER algorithm, we must calculate the "integral image". The value of a pixel in this integral image is the sum of the values of the pixels in the original image whose indices of position (column and row) are less than or equal to the indices of position of the pixel in question.

If:

– $i(x,y)$, the value of the pixels in the original image;

– $ii(x,y)$ the value of the pixels in the integral image;

then

$$ii(x, y) = \sum_{x'<x, y'<y} i(x', y') \qquad\qquad [6.29]$$

where $i(x, y)$ represents the pixel situated at the xth column and the yth row of the image I [BAY 06, VIO 01]. Let us take a very simple example based on 16 pixels. The original values of these pixels are given in Figure 6.18. Its integral image is shown in Figure 6.19.

1	1	1	1
1	4	1	1
1	1	1	4
1	1	1	1

Figure 6.18. *Example pixel values for an original image, for BOX FILTER calculations*

1	2	3	4
2	7	9	11
3	9	12	18
4	11	15	22

Figure 6.19. *Example integral image of BOX FILTER calculations*

Taking the second pixel of the first line in the integral image (2), it is the sum of the first pixel of the first line in the original image (1) and the second pixel of the first line in the original image (1).

Similarly, the second pixel of the second row of the integral image (7) is as follows:

= first pixel of the first row of the original image (1);

+ second pixel of the first row of the original image (1);

+ first pixel of the second row of the original image (1);

+ second pixel of the second row of the original image (4);

And so on for all the pixels of the integral image.

However, from a software point of view, it is preferable to use the recursive version that introduces a new matrix $s(x, y)$:

$$s(x,y) = s(x,y-1) + i(x,y)$$

$$ii(x,y) = ii(x-1,y) + s(x,y) \qquad\qquad [6.30]$$

where $s(x, -1) = 0$ and $ii(-1, y) = 0$ [VIO 01].

The integral image can thus be calculated in one reading of the original image.

6.2.2.3. *The sum and average of pixels on a rectangle*

Starting from the integral image, we can calculate the sum of the pixels on a rectangle. If we wish to calculate the sum of the pixels on the blue rectangle in Figure 6.20, we must calculate:

$$D- C- B+A \hspace{4cm} [6.31]$$

where D is the lower right value of the rectangle, C is the lower left value, B is the upper right value and A is the upper left value. If we return to our example and calculate the sum on the 2×2 square at upper left, we have for the integral image the corresponding square shown in Figure 6.21, where the values of A, B, C and D are displayed in red in bold, so A = 7, B = 9, C = 9 and D = 12.

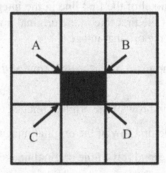

Figure 6.20. *Representation of the points to be summed for BOX FILTER. For a color version of this figure, see www.iste.co.uk/leroy/stereoscopy.zip*

1	2	3	4
2	7	9	11
3	9	12	18
4	11	15	22

Figure 6.21. *Representation of the summation process in BOX FILTER 1. For a color version of this figure, see www.iste.co.uk/leroy/stereoscopy.zip*

The sum of the pixels on the square is thus:

$$D–C–B+A = 12– 3– 3+1 = 7 \hspace{3cm} [6.32]$$

And we can verify this with the original image: $4+1+1+1 = 7$ (Figure 6.22).

	12–3–3+1 = 7	7	
	7	7	

Figure 6.22. *Representation of the summation process in BOX FILTER 2*

Of course for a 2×2 square, the benefit is fairly minimal, but when the rectangle becomes a little larger, this maneuver becomes more interesting.

Now that we have the sum of all the pixels on the rectangle, we can easily calculate the average on this rectangle by dividing by the number of pixels contained therein, that is 4 (Figure 6.23).

	7/4 = 1.75	1.75	
	1.75	1.75	

Figure 6.23. *Explanation of the averages in the BOX FILTER example*

6.2.2.4. High frequencies

At this stage, we are able to calculate the high frequencies of the image. We subtract the matrix of averages from the initial matrix (Figure 6.24).

We see that there was a high frequency in our original image, thus, in the high-frequency matrix, there is a relatively high number [2.25].

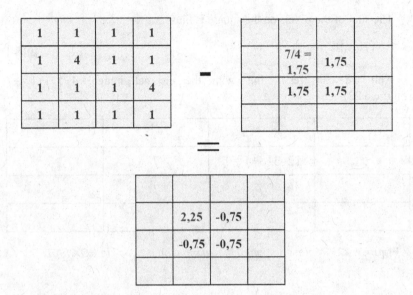

Figure 6.24. *High frequencies in the BOX FILTER calculation example*

6.2.2.5. *Reconstruction*

Normally, the algorithm stops here. We see that this poses a problem for the stated goal: suppressing high frequencies in some places. In fact, we know where the high frequencies are located, but the reconstruction of the image is not yet possible. For this, a slight modification has been made to the algorithm, not required for its original use.

Since we obtained the high frequencies by subtracting the matrix of averages from the initial image, it would be logical to suppose that by adding the high-frequency matrix to the low-frequency (average) matrix, we would retrieve the initial matrix (initial image) subject to the effects of nearby edges.

To apply this process to the image, we therefore suppress the unwanted high frequencies before adding the modified high-frequency image to the matrix of low frequencies to obtain the modified original image.

6.2.2.6. Multi-resolution

As discussed earlier, we performed decomposition and recomposition to detect high frequencies that show variations on 2-pixel-per-side squares of frequencies. However, we would also like to be able to do this for slightly lower frequencies. In effect, we want to keep the "multi-resolution" aspect that the wavelet transformation offered us. We will show below that it is still possible to obtain the same information.

It is interesting to consider that we obtained this matrix of high frequencies based on the average of a 2×2 pixel square. Thus, if we take a 4×4 pixel matrix, even 9×9 pixels, we will obtain averages calculated on a greater number of pixels, and therefore, a high-frequency matrix displaying lower and lower frequencies. The larger the rectangles of averages that we take, the more coarse the details displayed by the high-frequency matrix.

6.2.2.7. Result of the decompositions in images

This method gives us, in theory, usable images. But what exactly are the results that it can give? What do these matrices of low and high frequencies look like?

Figure 6.25 shows an image that we have already used as an example for the wavelet transform. We are going to calculate its integral image (which cannot be represented because the values of its "pixels" mostly exceed 255). Then, we will calculate the matrix of averages calculated over a 5-pixel square and the associated matrix of details.

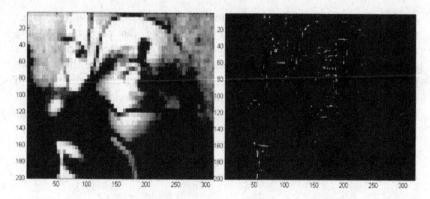

Figure 6.25. Decomposition into high and low frequencies with BOX FILTER on a 5-pixel square basis of calculation

Finally, we show the matrix of averages calculated over an 8-pixel square and its matrix of details (Figure 6.26).

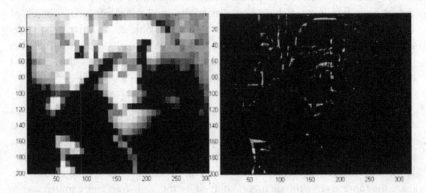

Figure 6.26. *Decomposition into high and low frequencies with BOX FILTER on an 8-pixel square basis of calculation*

We see that the images do indeed show a blurred image on the left, and another showing the details that have been eliminated on the right. We discuss in section 6.2.4.5 the link between blur and high frequencies.

6.2.3. *Using a rolling average and other "blurs"*

6.2.3.1. *Rolling average*

As we can see in the images in the earlier section, low-resolution images are "pixelated". To remove this jaggedness, we can perform a rolling average on the pixels. This means that we no longer replace the pixels on a square by averaging the values of pixels on that same square, but that we replace each pixel by the average calculated on a square surrounding the said pixel. Figure 6.28 shows the averages over 4 pixels calculated from Figure 6.27, as before.

In comparison, Figure 6.29 represents a rolling average carried out for a 2-pixel square. Applied to our working image and for an average carried out on a 2-pixel per side square, it gives us Figure 6.30, which is less jagged.

1	2	3	4	5	6
7	8	9	10	11	12
13	14	15	16	17	18
19	20	21	22	23	24
25	26	27	28	29	30
31	32	33	34	35	36

Figure 6.27. *Starting matrix for the difference in calculating averages*

4.5	4.5	6.5	6.5	8.5	8.5
4.5	4.5	6.5	6.5	8.5	8.5
16.5	16.5	18.5	18.5	20.5	20.5
16.5	16.5	18.5	18.5	20.5	20.5
28.5	28.5	30.5	30.5	32.5	32.5
28.5	28.5	30.5	30.5	32.5	32.5

Figure 6.28. *Calculating averages over squares of pixels*

4.5	5.5	6.5	7.5	8.5	6
10.5	11.5	12.5	13.5	14.5	12
16.5	17.5	18.5	19.5	12.5	18
22.5	23.5	24.5	25.5	26.5	24
28.5	29.5	30.5	31.5	32.5	30
31	32	33	34	35	36

Figure 6.29. *Calculating rolling averages*

6.2.3.2. *Other "blurs"*

We see that Figure 6.30 is still slightly cloudy. To solve this problem, we can apply filters that are less "square". Among these, there are quadratic and Gaussian filters. They are both calculated in the same way as rolling averages and are thus carried out on the graphics card and not on the motherboard (see section 6.2.4.3). What distinguishes them from rolling averages is the weight accorded to the pixels on the edges of the base of calculation.

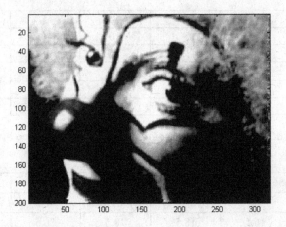

Figure 6.30. *Rolling averages over 2-pixel-per-side squares*

6.2.3.2.1. Quadratic filters

Equation

This filter gives a weighting to the pixels of the base with respect to the square of the distance to the pixel being treated. We thus calculate the distance between the pixel being treated and the pixels composing the base of calculation.

DEFINITION 6.5.– *If (X_{calcul}, Y_{calcul}) is the position in row and column of the pixel being treated and (X, Y) is the position in row and column of a pixel in the base of calculation, we define the distance between these two pixels:*

$$d = \sqrt{(X_{calcul} - X)^2 + (Y_{calcul} - Y)^2} \qquad [6.33]$$

We give each pixel in the base of calculation a weight:

$$1 - d^2/r^2 \quad \text{if } 1 - d^2/r^2 > 0 \qquad [6.34]$$

0 Otherwise

where r represents the number of pixels per side of the square of the base of calculation.

Next, we add the values of the pixels multiplied by their weight and we divide this value by the sum of all the weights of the pixels in question. This gives us the value of the pixel being treated.

Result

Figure 6.31 represents the rolling quadratic average carried out with $r = 4$, as shown in Figure 6.7. We see that the cloudiness is greatly reduced, but still present.

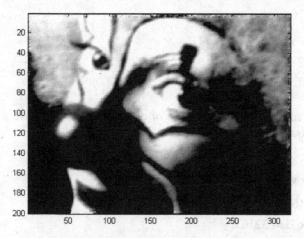

Figure 6.31. *Rolling quadratic average carried out on a 4-pixel-per-side base of calculation*

Remarks

This kind of blur is quite practical to use, but yet still carries quite a heavy calculation load, notably because of the calculation of the distance that involves a square root.

6.2.3.2.2. Gaussian filters

Equation

This filter gives weights to the pixels of the base following a Gaussian function in two dimensions centered on the pixel being treated. If r represents the number of pixels per side of the square of the base of calculation, the pixel being treated has a weight of 2^{r-1}. The other weights are also powers of two. The weakest powers are zero ($2^0 = 1$) and they increase as we approach the basis of calculation.

We can write the distribution of weights for a calculation base of r pixels per side:

$$\begin{pmatrix} 2^0 & 2^1 & & & 2^1 & 2^0 \\ 2^1 & 2^2 & & & 2^2 & 2^1 \\ & & & & & \\ & & 2^{r-1} & & & \\ & & & & & \\ 2^1 & 2^2 & & & 2^1 & 2^0 \\ 2^0 & 2^1 & & & 2^2 & 2^0 \end{pmatrix} \qquad [6.35]$$

Thus, for a 7-pixel square base of calculation, we will have a matrix of weights equal to:

$$\begin{array}{l} 1\ 2\ 48421 \\ 2\ 4\ 8\ 16\ 842 \\ 4\ 8163216\ 84 \\ 8163264\ 3216\ 8 \\ 4\ 816\ 32\ 16\ 84 \\ 2\ 4\ 816842 \\ 1\ 2\ 4\ 8\ 421 \end{array} \qquad [6.36]$$

Then, we add the values of the pixels multiplied by their weight and we divide this value by the sum of all the weights of the pixels in question. This gives us the value of the pixel being treated.

Result

Figure 6.32 represents the rolling Gaussian average calculated with $r = 4$, as shown in Figure 6.7. We see that the cloudiness is even more reduced.

Remarks

This type of blur is often used in image processing, notably in industrial software. Its base-2 calculation makes it very easy to calculate.

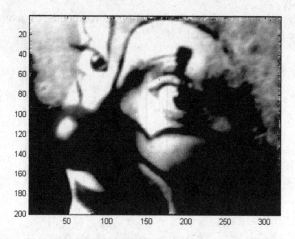

Figure 6.32. *Rolling Gaussian average calculated on a 5-pixel-per-side base*

6.2.4. *Comparison of algorithms*

6.2.4.1. *Haar wavelets/BOX FILTER comparison*

6.2.4.1.1. Mathematical comparison

We showed in section 6.2.1.3 that the Haar wavelet is the fastest to calculate. It is also the easiest to use and intuitively understand.

The low-pass filter of the Haar wavelet is: $fb = [0.5, 0.5]$ and the high-pass filter is $fh = [0.5, -0.5]$. This means that, when we perform the numerical convolution of signal s using the low-pass filter, we obtain:

$$x[n] = s[n] * fb[2] + s[n+1] * fb[1] \tag{6.37}$$

$$x[n] = s[n] * 0.5 + s[n+1] * 0.5 \tag{6.38}$$

This corresponds to the average of the datum $s[n]$ and the following datum $s[n+1]$. The convolution of this low-pass filter and an arbitrary signal is shown in Figure 6.33.

The signal is represented by the bold line, while the convolution of the signal by the low-pass filter is represented by the dotted blue line. We thus see that the Haar wavelet transformation corresponds to averaging two consecutive points of the signal.

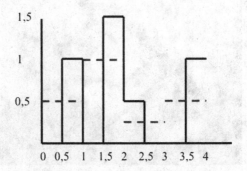

Figure 6.33. *Example of calculation of Haar wavelet transform*

6.2.4.1.2. Another comparison

Differences in principle

Remember that the fast wavelet transform is recursive. To obtain frequencies showing details over 16 pixels, we must first calculate the details over 2 pixels, over 4, then over 8 before calculating them over 16 pixels. Let us note now that this is not necessary with this new algorithm, since to get details over 16 pixels, it is enough to calculate the matrix of averages on 16 pixels, which takes no more time than the average on 2 pixels (because of the integral image).

Moreover, since in our algorithm the original image is retrieved by adding the matrices of averages and details, whatever the level of detail in question, the reconstruction is not recursive either. It is not necessary to calculate all levels of detail. We only need to calculate the level that interests us.

Note as well that for our reconstruction, it is unnecessary to reconstruct the whole image. Imagine that only a tiny segment of the image interests us – let us say, a 9 × 9 pixel square. We only modify this section in the matrix of details, the rest of the image remaining unchanged. As we never modify the matrix of low frequencies, the sum of these two is identical to the original image everywhere, except on the small square being modified. It is thus not useful to carry out this addition elsewhere than on the square in question, since, elsewhere, we can preserve the pixels of the original image.

Let us note also that if we want to calculate the details on 9 × 11 or 9 × 6 pixel rectangles, we can do so perfectly well. The rectangle of calculation adjusts immediately. This type of calculation is not possible with wavelets, because the details are always calculated on squares of 2^i, $i \in \Re > 0$ pixels per side for reasons of orthogonality.

In contrast, we lose some information on the direction of frequencies with banks of filters, compared to wavelets. For example, we no longer have the three matrices of high frequencies in horizontal, vertical and diagonal directions. We could retrieve the vertical high frequencies by calculating the matrices of low frequencies on rectangles of width equal to that of the image and of height corresponding to the degree of detail. The matrix of horizontal details would be obtained in the same way, but we cannot obtain the matrix of diagonal high frequencies.

Differences in time

We changed the algorithm so as to gain calculation time. Let us see now if this new algorithm effectively fulfills this expectation. To be able to compare calculation times between the fast wavelet transform and the BOX FILTER algorithm, we must use comparable treatments. If we need four iterations of the wavelet algorithm to arrive at a level of detail of 16 pixels, we nevertheless get levels of detail of 2, 4 and 8 pixels at the same time. So, we will have to calculate levels of detail of 2, 4, 8 and finally 16 pixels for the BOX FILTER algorithm to obtain the same information. Table 6.1 shows relative calculation times between the wavelet transform and BOX FILTER. The two algorithms have thus performed four decompositions and recompositions each.

Size of image	Relative time (wav/box)
216 × 216	1.937
512 × 512	17.733
1,024 × 1,024	9.945

Table 6.1. *Relative time for image treatment using wavelet transform and BOX FILTER*

Now that we know that the BOX FILTER algorithm is much faster, it would be interesting to know if it calculates decompositions and recompositions in real time. This time, we will only perform one decomposition and recomposition of the whole image. The results in images per second are shown in Table 6.2.

Size of image	Number of images per second
512 × 512	66
1,024 × 1,024	16

Table 6.2. *Number of images per second for a BOX FILTER decomposition and recomposition of an image in terms of its size*

Note that for an image of 1,024 × 1,024 we are not yet in real time. In contrast, for a 512 × 512 image, we have passed the 50 images per second required for stereoscopy. However, we must take account of the treatment and transformation of RGB to YUV encoding. Moreover, in practice, the image must be transferred from the graphics card to the motherboard (we will see why later). These two operations quadruple the calculation time for 1,024 × 1,024 images.

6.2.4.2. *Comparison of BOX FILTER/average on graphics card*

6.2.4.2.1. Mathematical and experimental comparison

We have seen that the BOX FILTER algorithm calculates averages over squares of several pixels per side. It is thus to be expected that the results of these algorithms will be equivalent since, by definition, the algorithm running on the graphics cards calculates averages on squares of pixels. We can, nevertheless, show the results obtained with this algorithm to ensure that, experimentally, we do arrive at the same images. Figure 6.34 is the result of an average calculated over squares of 2 pixels per side. Figure 6.35 is the result of an average calculated over squares of 4 pixels per side.

Let us perform the same calculation of similarities between these images and those obtained by the BOX FILTER algorithm to verify if this resemblance is more than just visual. We obtain for the averages calculated over squares of 2 and 4 pixels, compared to the BOX FILTER algorithm for the same resolution: 0! Which means that there is no difference between the digital approximations.

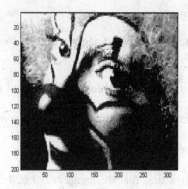

Figure 6.34. *Decomposition with an average over squares of 2 pixels per side*

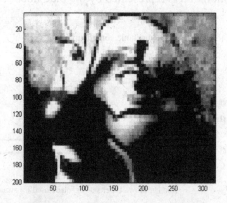

Figure 6.35. *Decomposition with an average over squares of 4 pixels per side*

6.2.4.2.2. Preamble on algorithmic complexity: BOX FILTER/average

Let us calculate the complexity for averages performed over squares of n pixels per side in images containing $N \times M$ pixels.

Algorithm for averàges

For each small square, we must make $n \times n$ additions and one division: n^2+1. We must carry out this operation as many times as there are squares in the image MN/n^2.

So our complexity $= (n^2 + 1) \times MN/n^2$.

BOX FILTER algorithm

We must calculate the integral image: we need two additions for each pixel (with the recursion formula): $2MN$.

For each average square, we need four additions and a division: $4 + 1$.

Multiply this by the number of squares in the image MN/n^2.

So we have total complexity: $2MN + 5MN/n^2$.

These two complexities for an image of $1,024 \times 1,024$ pixels are illustrated in Figure 6.36. The complexity of the algorithm of averages as a function of n is represented by the red line, while the complexity of BOX FILTER as a function of n is represented by the blue line.

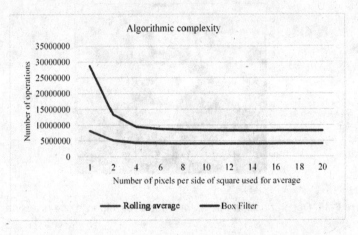

Figure 6.36. *Complexity of BOX FILTER and averages in relation to size of calculation square for a 1,024 × 1,024 image. For a color version of this figure, see www.iste.co.uk/leroy/stereoscopy.zip*

We see that for jagged images, thus corresponding to a Haar decomposition, the complexity is lower during direct calculation of the average compared to BOX FILTER.

6.2.4.2.3. Complexity for rolling algorithms

Rolling averages algorithm

For each small square, we need $n \times n$ additions and one division: $n^2 + 1$.

This operation must be carried out as many times are there are pixels in the image: *MN*

So we have an overall complexity: $(n^2+1) \times MN$.

BOX FILTER algorithm

We calculate the integral image: for each pixel, two additions are required (with the recursion formula): $2MN$.

For each square of averages,we need four additions and one division: $4 + 1$.

Multiply this by the number of pixels in the image: *MN*.

So we have an overall complexity: $2MN + 5MN = 7MN$.

It is a constant complexity.

These two complexities for an image of 1,024 × 1,024 pixels are shown in Figure 6.37. The complexity of the algorithm of averages as a function of *n* is shown in red, while the complexity of BOX FILTER as a function of *n* is shown in blue. We see that very quickly the BOX FILTER algorithm performs much better in complexity and thus in speed.

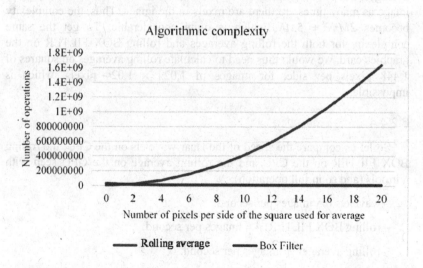

Figure 6.37. *Complexity for rolling BOX FILTER and rolling averages as a function of the size of the calculation square for a 1,024 × 1,024 image. For a color version of this figure, see www.iste.co.uk/leroy/stereoscopy.zip*

6.2.4.3. *Difference in algorithm for different media*

So then, what is the attraction of the rolling average algorithm if its complexity explodes in relation to the number of pixels over which the average is calculated? The complexities calculated earlier give a false picture of the difference in calculation time for these processes, because they are not carried out on the same media. In fact, the rolling BOX FILTER algorithm is calculated on the motherboard (the CPU) while the rolling averages algorithm is calculated on the graphics card (the GPU). Now, speed of memory access to the graphics card or the motherboard cannot be compared. To carry out the calculation on the motherboard processor, we must first transfer the images from the graphics card to the motherboard, carry out the calculation and resend the processed image to the graphics card for display. Now, if the time taken to send data from the processor to the graphics card is relatively low, it is quite different going the other way.

Why not perform the BOX FILTER process on the graphics card? Simply, because a graphics card program is executed as many times are there are pixels in parallel. In addtion, starting from a pixel, it is easy to access neighboring pixels or even those somewhat further away, but quite difficult to access pixels across the whole image. Now, for the BOX FILTER algorithm, we must calculate the integral image before calculating the averages. So, on the graphics card, we would need to recalculate an integral image as many times are there are pixels in the image. Thus, the complexity becomes $2M^2N^2 + 5MN$, which is quite considerable. To get the same complexity for both the rolling averages and rolling BOX FILTER on the graphics card, we would thus need to calculate rolling averages on squares of 1,448 pixels per side, for images of 1,024 × 1,024 pixels, which is impossible.

6.2.4.4. *Time difference*

So let us compare the speed of the Haar wavelets on the CPU, the rolling BOX FILTER on the CPU and the rolling average on the GPU seen with Virtools (and so in full operation):

– wavelets 0.5 images per second;

– rolling BOX FILTER: 4.6 images per second;

– rolling average: 97 images per second.

6.2.4.5. *Link between blur and high frequencies*

The rolling average technique gives us "blurred" images, of course. But we might also wonder if rendering an image blurry actually corresponds to the suppression of high frequencies. At first, we would be tempted to reply "yes", but let us verify this intuitive response. To do this, let us run the given images through our rolling average and Fourier transform algorithms.

Let us put a threshold on the Fourier transform of the initial image to better highlight the spatial frequencies present. In Figure 6.38, we see that there are many high frequencies in our initial image.

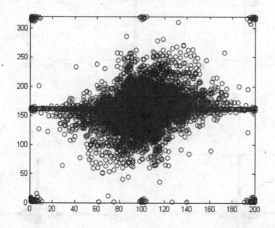

Figure 6.38. *Putting a threshold on the Fourier transform of the initial image*

Let us see the same thresholding on the Fourier transform of the image obtained by the rolling average method over 2 pixels on our clown (Figure 6.39). Note that just performing the rolling average over these very small squares already removes many high frequencies. As an example, we can show the same threshold for squares of 4, 8, 16 and 32 pixels per side in Figure 6.40.

We see that the greater the number of pixels over which the rolling average is performed, the more the high frequencies disappear. For each of these rolling averages, we can calculate the highest frequency present. To characterize this frequency, we will not use cycles per degree of ocular vision, since we do not know how far away the eye is located. However, we can compare them to the period (expressed in pixels) of the corresponding sine curve.

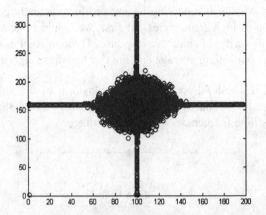

Figure 6.39. *Thresholding of the Fourier transform of the rolling average over 2-pixel-per-side squares*

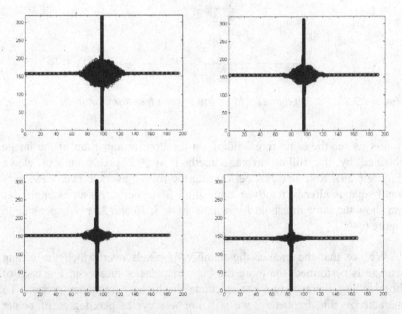

Figure 6.40. *Thresholding of the Fourier decomposition for rolling averages over 4, 8, 16 and 32 pixels (left-to-right and top-to-bottom)*

Number of pixels for the rolling average	Period of remaining oscillations in vertical pixels	Period of remaining oscillations in horizontal pixels
2	6.5	3.5
4	7	7.5
8	14	8
16	17	14
32	24	17.5

Table 6.3. *Correspondence between the number of periods of remaining oscillations and the number of pixels for the rolling average*

6.2.4.6. *Overall comparison*

In Table 6.4, we sum up the different properties of the three algorithms. Those which are or may be interesting are in green. We have thus decided to use rolling average calculations on the GPU. In fact, this is the only method that allows us to perform our calculations in real time. However, the wavelet transform could be very interesting because of its direct link with frequencies. We have managed to overcome this gap for calculations of "blur" on the GPU, but a direct link would have been more intuitive. Furthermore, Chapter 1 showed the link between wavelets and our visual system, and it would have been more sensible to keep this link. The BOX FILTER algorithm would have been a good alternative with respect to the wavelet transformation in terms of speed, if we had stayed on the CPU. It would have allowed us to address only a single zone very easily. In fact, if we only want to deal with the periphery of the screen, it would very easily be possible with this algorithm, thus reducing the processing of images.

Criterion	Wavelets	Box filter	GPU
Number of images processed in Virtools per second	0.5	4.6	97
Real time	No	No	Yes
Decomposition	Whole image	Whole image	Per object
Recomposition	Whole image	Whole image	Per object
Choice of "blur"	Yes	No	Yes
Direct link with frequencies	Yes	No	No

Table 6.4. *Comparison of the three algorithms studied*

6.2.5. *Chosen solution*

We chose the blur algorithm on the graphics card performed with a rolling average so as to be able to carry out processing in real time. Adaptive blur was calculated according to Perrin's function (see section 3.3.2): for $C(d,f)$ the visual comfort, where f is the spatial frequency present and d is the disparity:

$$C(d, f) = a(d - d_0 - kf^{k'})$$ [6.39]

The interpolation parameters are as follows:

$a = -0.010$

$d_0 = 18.9$ [6.40]

$k = 221.1$

$k' = -0.74$

We can thus calculate the maximum frequency for a given level of comfort:

$$f = \sqrt[k']{\frac{1}{ka}(ad - ad_0 - C(f,d))}$$ [6.41]

We consider that the comfort must be at least equal to 0. To calculate the acceptable frequency by means of equation [6.39], we lack the disparity d or the horizontal parallax. This is calculated from the position of the subject and the position of the virtual point (Figure 6.41).

Because of the relationships of similar triangles, we can write:

$$Horizontal\ Parallax = \frac{Distance\ Object * DIO}{(Distance\ Object - Distance\ Eye)}$$ [6.42]

We therefore now know the maximum frequency acceptable at a point. However, a graphics card program only considers pixels and not spatial frequency. We will have to express our spatial frequency (in cycles by degree of visual angle) in pixels (Figure 6.42).

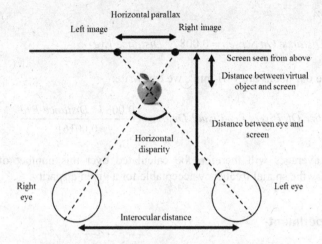

Figure 6.41. *Calculation of horizontal parallax*

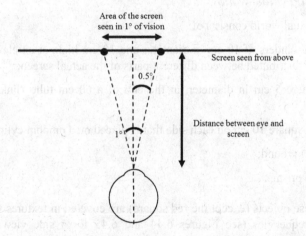

Figure 6.42. *Calculation of number of pixels per degree of visual angle*

We start from the visual half-angle so as to use the trigonometric relationships in a triangle–rectangle:

$$\tan(\frac{1°}{2}) = \frac{Distance\ On\ Screen\ /\ 2}{Distance\ Eye} \qquad [6.43]$$

Thus:

$$Distance\ On\ Screen = 0.0087 * Distance\ Eye \qquad\qquad [6.44]$$

and since our pixels are 1.61 mm^2, we can write:

$$Number\ Of\ Pixels\ Per\ Visual\ Degree = \frac{0.0087 * Distance\ Eye}{0.00161} \qquad [6.45]$$

The averages will therefore be calculated over this number of pixels divided by the spatial frequency acceptable for a given disparity.

6.3. Experiment

6.3.1. *The task*

6.3.1.1. *The virtual world*

Our virtual world consists of:

– five cylinders of 10 cm in diameter and 20 cm high, at an elevation of 80 cm and distributed between different parts of the actual screen;

– a sphere 5 cm in diameter, at the end of a 60 cm tube "linked" to a WiiMote;

– a red square 10 cm on each side that is placed on a random cylinder;

– a background;

– three prisms.

All these objects (except the red square) are covered in textures very rich in high frequencies (see Figures 6.44 and 6.45 for a side view without textures).

6.3.1.2. *The "object of the game"*

The red square will be placed on a cylinder chosen in a random fashion (without resampling). The subject is asked to place the bottom of the sphere tangentially to the red square, to hold this position for 2 sec, then to place the center of the sphere at the center of the red square. They then wait 2 sec again, then press the "A" button on the WiiMote.

Figure 6.43. *The virtual world. For a color version of this figure, see www.iste.co.uk/leroy/stereoscopy.zip*

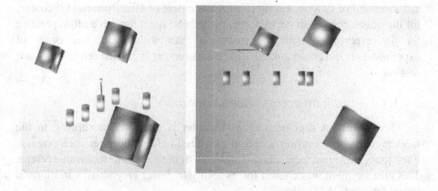

Figure 6.44. *Virtual world without textures, seen front on and from the side*

When the "A" button is pressed, the square "chooses" another cylinder, while the previous cylinder moves horizontally from left to right in a random direction and at a random speed, but in a given time (3 sec). In this way, the subject cannot memorize the placement of the cylinders. However, this movement is canceled if there is a risk that the cylinder will move outside the field of vision. The red square will rest on each cylinder 50 times. This game is a question of accuracy, not of speed. Thus, the subject can take as much time as they wish before counting their 2 sec, to be sure of getting a good position. This game lasts around 30 min.

This task was chosen because it allows us to concentrate the subject's attention for a certain period of time on objects situated in one part or another of the screen, so as to direct the gaze toward different disparities. It includes a measure of accuracy that allows us to verify if our processing reduces the effectiveness of a subject performing a task. Finally, this "game" resembles a load-handling operation that a worker might carry out in a virtual environment (in training, for example).

6.4. Measurements of fatigue taken

6.4.1. *Objective measurements*

6.4.1.1. *Effectiveness of the task*

We measure the error in distance between the center of the sphere and the center of the square when the "A" button of the WiiMote is pressed, as well as the time taken to complete the task. This is not strictly speaking a measurement of fatigue, but more a measurement of effectiveness. Of course, for this measurement to be valuable, the subject must not have more practice for the experiment with the treatment than without it. The order of experiments is thus randomized. This measurement is carried out during each session.

6.4.1.1.1. Proximum accommodation function

The proximum accommodation function is measured according to the rules mentioned in section 5.2. It is measured before and after each session. Each time, two measurements are taken (with both eyes) to make an average. This measurement was chosen for its ability to detect very small variations in visual fatigue [LAM 09].

6.4.1.1.2. Ease of accommodation

Ease of accommodation is measured according to the rules mentioned in section 5.3. However, we carry this out for more than 1 min for greater precision. It is measured before and after each session.

6.4.1.1.3. Stereoscopic acuity

Stereoscopic acuity is measured using Wirt points (see section 5.4). It is measured before and after each session. This technique was chosen due to the very wide range of acuities measured and their level of precision.

6.4.1.2. *Subjective measurements*

Subjective measurements are presented in the form of questions posed to the subject after the two virtual worlds have been experienced. There are a total of three questions as follows:

1) Which world was the most a esthetically pleasing?

2) Was the task easier than last time?

3) Was the task more tiring than last time?

6.4.2. **Procedure**

The test was performed on two different days; one day for the test without image treatment and another with it. This spacing was necessary so that fatigue from the first test did not influence the second, whatever the order in which they were presented. The two days were not necessarily consecutive.

When the subject arrived, they tossed a coin to see if they would start with the scene treated against fatigue or with the untreated scene. The accommodative and stereoscopic tests were carried out and the simulation began. The rules were explained. The subject was asked to signal when they were ready. They carried out the task (Figure 6.45), then the accommodative and stereoscopic measurements were retaken, so as to compare with the measurements taken before the task. The second test was carried out after an eye rest of at least 24 h. Visual and stereoscopic acuities were remeasured before beginning the test.

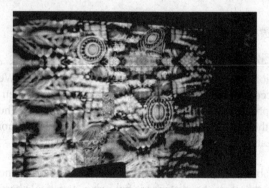

Figure 6.45. *Subject performing the non-blurred task. For a color version of this figure, see www.iste.co.uk/leroy/stereoscopy.zip*

6.4.3. *The subjects*

The subjects chosen were all between 20 and 40 years of age. This upper limit was set so that presbyopia would not complicate the accommodative measurements, particularly ease of accommodation [BEN 07]. Subjects might present visual problems such as myopia or astigmatism on condition that they wear their visual correction (glasses or contact lenses). No subject presented any problems with stereoscopy. Results are given for a panel of 20 people, mostly male (85%).

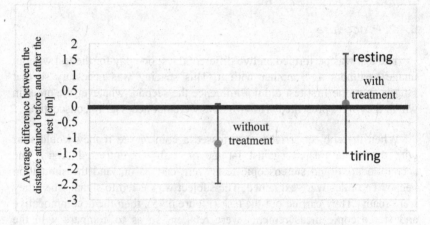

Figure 6.46. *Change in the proximum accommodation function*

6.5. Result

6.5.1. *Proximum accommodation function*

Figure 6.46 shows the difference in the measurements of proximum accommodation function taken before and after each task. We see that the proximum accommodation function barely changes at all when we apply the treatment of progressive suppression of spatial frequencies. When the latter is not applied, the subjects lose 1.21 cm. Their eyes are thus more tired when our image treatment is not applied.

The probability associated with the significance of differences in average is 99.6%, and therefore this distance is not just a statistical aberration.

6.5.2. *Ease of accommodation*

Figure 6.47 shows the differences in relative time elapsed between the number of semi-cycles of the lens apparatus shown in Figure 5.4, before and after the task. As we can see, the difference is on average 1.77 semi-cycles per minute. The relative times elapsed between semi-cycles follow a normal distribution. This difference is significant since the probability of significance associated with it is 99.45%.

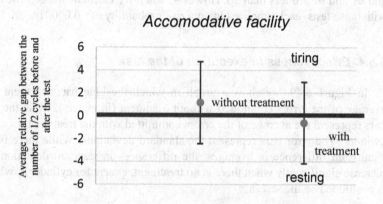

Figure 6.47. *Change in accommodative facility*

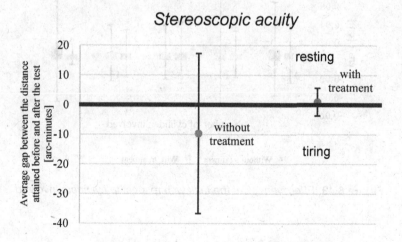

Figure 6.48. *Change in stereoscopic acuity*

6.5.3. *Stereoscopic acuity*

In Figure 6.48, we see that the difference in gap for stereoscopic acuity is quite important. Stereoscopic acuity seems to be significantly diminished when our treatment is not applied and, vice versa, it does not seem to change when our algorithm modifies the image.

However, it must be noted that this distribution is unfortunately not normal. The difference between the two standard deviations is significant, and $n1$ and $n2$ are less than 30. However, when we calculate the significance with these tests, each time we obtain a risk probability of <0.00001.

6.5.4. *Effectiveness in execution of the task*

In Figure 6.49, we show a graph in which the blue bars represent the average of the errors committed without treatment (in meters), while the red bars represent the average of the errors committed with the treatment for each cylinder. The error bars represent the standard deviations. While there is no significant difference in averages, the differences in standard deviation all increase significantly when there is no treatment, except for cylinder 3, which is positioned on the screen.

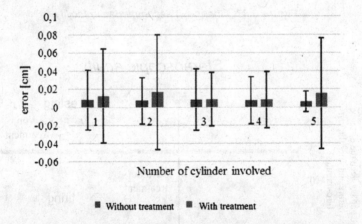

Figure 6.49. *Effectiveness of the task with respect to cylinders involved*

6.5.5. Subjective measurements

In Figure 6.50, we see that the subjects prefer the untreated world from an esthetic point of view. Note that practically one-third of subjects questioned did not see any difference between one day and the other.

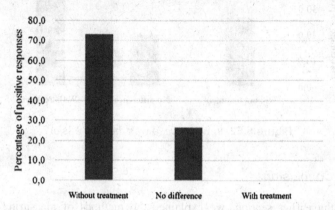

Figure 6.50. *Which case was the more aesthetically pleasing?*

In Figure 6.51, we can see that twice as many subjects experienced the world without our adaptive treatment as more fatiguing than the world without it. This rather tends to confirm the results of the tests of visual fatigue which we performed in the earlier sections. In Figure 6.52, we see that the subjects also found the task easier when the virtual world was given our image treatment.

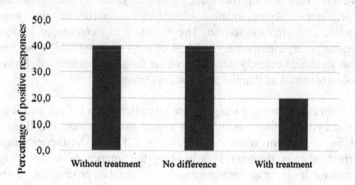

Figure 6.51. *In which case was the task more tiring for your eyes?*

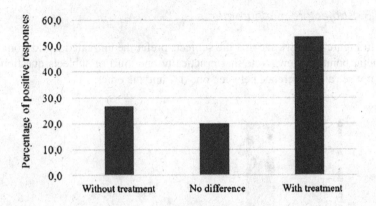

Figure 6.52. *In which case was the task easier?*

6.5.6. *Conclusions*

In the earlier section, we explained the methods of measuring visual fatigue as well as our test protocol. We showed that treating the image with adaptive blur reduces visual fatigue in stereoscopic vision. However, it somewhat decreases the effectiveness of the task, as well as the aesthetic aspect of the virtual world. In Chapter 7, we will discuss our results and test protocol.

6.5.7. *Discussion*

We have seen that our treatment significantly reduces the deterioration of the proximum accommodation function, as well as the ease of accommodation after immersion. The reduction in stereoscopic acuity after immersion is very significantly reduced, or even removed. This tends to show that our treatment actually decreases visual fatigue in immersion. Moreover, our subjects remarked that the task was less tiring.

In contrast, the treated images were less pleasing to the eye and less well accepted by the subjects, even if they agreed that they were less tiring. This could be a problem when aesthetics are a factor. Aesthetics might be important when a designer is inspecting the interior of a car using our application. It is also important for an artistic production, a public demonstration, or when the user needs to assess the finishing of their product.

We saw that the accuracy of the task was not reduced. The average error did not change. In contrast, its standard deviation increased, so the accuracy of the task was affected. On the other hand, many subjects stated that the task was easier when the image was treated against visual fatigue

6.5.7.1. *To treat the materials or treat the image?*

The treatment carried out on the graphics card is carried out on each object, whereas treatments by wavelets or by BOX FILTER are carried out over the whole image. We are therefore entitled to wonder about the implications of such a difference. We thus ran two programs on the graphics card, one working material by material (or object by object), and the other treating the whole image in post-treatment (as a texture). It is quite logical to think that there would be no notable differences if there are very few objects (as in the world used for our test of the influence of our treatment), and the differences between the two would be minor. In contrast, in a world containing many different objects (or objects composed of different materials), the differences are much more visible. Note that this is often the case in virtual worlds: for example, a car interior consists of a great number of small objects (buttons, handles, grids, etc.). It is therefore interesting to make this comparison with a world more complex than that of "the test". Nevertheless, it would be easier to compare these two methods in a relatively regular world.

To illustrate this difference, we apply the two methods to a world where the number of materials is very large. This world is represented in Figure 6.53: it consists of a fleet of spacecraft. The advantage of this world is that it is composed of many small identical vessels, which themselves composed of three different materials: the cockpit, the hull and the wings. These two latter materials are covered in textures containing very high frequencies. We can thus appreciate the differences on the nearby small objects. It also contains a larger vessel, which is composed of a single material.

6.5.7.1.1. Treating the materials

We begin by applying the algorithm material by .material. We see in Figure 6.54 that the high textures of the objects have been blurred, but the outlines of the materials remain very clear; for example, the cockpit of the first small vessel (very blurred) has a very sharp outline. The zero disparities are located on the fourth small vessel, which is not blurred. We also see that we have not applied our treatment to the starry background.

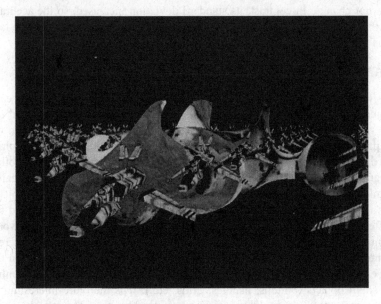

Figure 6.53. *Initial image*

One advantage is that, if one of the objects is important, we can decide not to apply the treatment to it. In our case, we have decided to not apply it to the background, for example,but any object could equally not be treated. This is notably important when there is an object that must be modified in detail by an operator (in an industrial context) or an object that must be highlighted to guide the eyes of the observer (in a gaming or artistic context).

Another advantage of this technique is to preserve the sharpness of the outlines. In fact, if the task is to count the number of vessels, it is still possible with this method; we can make the differences clear between each object. Moreover, it is easier to perceive the depth of an object if its outlines are clear, the disparities of the edges not being completely erased. In addition, the fact that this may be less "aesthetic" is less obvious.

There are unfortunately some disadvantages with this method. Since the difference between the objects remains marked, if there are many small objects, there are many high frequencies due to "breaks" between these objects. In our case, we have many small vessels in the background and their wings create high frequencies.

Figure 6.54. *Treating object by object*

Another disadvantage is that this treatment is difficult to manage for a user. In fact, this treatment must be applied over all the materials. So, every time a user introduces a new material, they must apply the treatment. This could quickly prove restrictive when there are many materials, as in virtual worlds that are a bit more complex. In addition, the more materials, the heavier the burden of processing is. In fact, it also treats the hidden parts of objects.

6.5.7.1.2. Treating the image

In Figure 6.55, we show the treatment carried out over the whole image. The non-blurred area also occurs at the level of the fourth small vessel. In contrast to the other method, the small vessels are no longer discernable after the fifth or sixth vessel. This corresponds better to a real situation of blur due to depth.

One of the advantages is the certainty of suppressing all the high frequencies at once. Indeed, we see in Figure 6.55 that there are no remaining high frequencies, either in the background or in the foreground, independent of the number of objects or materials to be treated.

Figure 6.55. *Treating the whole image*

The great advantage for users is that this treatment can be added very easily to an existing application. The programmer is not obliged to take the program into account from the outset. Moreover, the treatment is only applied once for the whole virtual world and does not treat hidden objects. This solution is thus much quick+er in both installation and functioning, especially if there is a large number of objects.

We cannot make an exception for an important or aesthetic object, since the treatment is not applied object by object. This also means that if an operator must carry out a precision task on one part of the virtual world, it absolutely must be located on the screen so as not to be blurred.

Objects in the background are no longer discernible at all. We see in Figure 6.55 that after the sixth small vessel we can no longer distinguish them, while the rows are eight vessels long. This means that, if the task consists of counting objects, it is totally impossible.

In addition, from an aesthetic point of view, the users notice the difference much more quickly, since the objects blur into each other. For example, the border between the large vessel and the sky is very weak in certain places.

6.5.7.2. *Conclusions*

Our experiments have shown that our treatment reduces visual fatigue, but somewhat reduces the aesthetic aspect of the virtual world. We also discussed the method to apply to suppress high frequencies, material by material or over the whole image at once. We have dealt with the advantages and disadvantages of both methods.

Reducing the Distance Between the Virtual Cameras

7.1. Principle

We have seen that stereoscopy can be fatiguing, and that this may be linked to overly marked disparities (see section 3.2). However, these disparities may be reduced if we reduce the distance between the virtual cameras. In fact, if we reduce this distance, the differences between the two images are lessened; the disparities decrease, as does the perception of depth by stereoscopy. At the extreme, if the distance between the virtual cameras is zero, we return to monoscopic vision.

I have often done this experiment with my students, during demonstrations in class. They were introduced to a virtual world in an immersive hall. They had stereoscopic vision in the beginning, but also motion parallax (see section 7.2.1.2) and all the other monoscopic cues (see section 7.2.1.1). After a while, I began progressively reducing the distance between the cameras. After some minutes, I asked them if they had noticed that the stereoscopy was no longer in operation. Out of almost 200 students, not even one had noticed that the stereoscopy had been eliminated. Some were still marveling over the 3 dimensions when I announced that there had been no stereoscopy for more than 5 min. I performed this experiment with the entirely pedagogic aim of showing them that stereoscopy is interesting, but not at all essential. Moreover, it is not the principal cue for depth perception. However, in view of the overwhelming majority of students who did not notice when the 3D was stopped, even having seen their classmates going through the same experiment, I began to wonder if this would not be an interesting way to reduce fatigue while still preserving the impressive side of demonstrations of stereoscopy.

7.1.1. *Usefulness of stereoscopy in depth perception*

We saw in section 7.4.2 that stereoscopy is one cue for depth perception, but not the only one. We wanted to verify the importance of this cue compared to others, and notably compared to motion parallax in an immersive hall. To measure this importance, we tried to quantify the perception of curvature in immersion using different types of immersion to verify which cues were the most significant in the perception of curves.

7.1.1.1. *Protocol*

7.1.1.1.1. The subjects

15 subjects underwent tests of perception of a sphere, while 18 people were tested on an unspecified shape. The subjects had to be in good health. They might have vision problems (myopia, astigmatism, farsightedness, presbyopia), as long as they wore corrective lenses. They had to be capable of moving around the room with no inconvenience. The interocular distance was measured for each subject and integrated into calculation of the virtual images when stereoscopy was being used.

All subjects needed to verify that they had good binocular vision. A simple screening test was carried out before the perception test itself: the subject was shown two adjacent cubes of different dimensions, with one significantly closer than the other. The person had to determine which was closer, three times in a row to eliminate guesswork.

7.1.1.1.2. Method used

The method we used was that of constant stimuli. This is in fact the most reliable and the most precise method [BON 86].

We looked for a differentiation threshold ("do you perceive the same virtual object as the physical object?"), and therefore used for our initial shape the virtual object corresponding to the real object. We identified a set of seven variations in each dimension (width, height, thickness) centered around the dimensions of the original object. We used an arithmetic progression rule for ease of use. Each stimulus was displayed three times by random sampling without replacement.

7.1.2. *The objects*

7.1.2.1. *The sphere*

7.1.2.1.1. The real sphere

The real sphere (Figure 7.2) was in reality a smooth plastic balloon with a diameter of 20 cm, painted green to match the color of the virtual model. It was shown in front of a black backdrop and lit in the same way as the virtual model (lamp arranged at the same location and intensity adjusted by hand by the experimenter, for the best possible correspondence, Figure 7.1). We tried to take films or photos of the two spheres to get the best comparison of luminosity. However, since the screen was rear projected, the sensor was saturated and could not take a photo showing what the eye perceived, as too much bias was induced by these sensors.

The distance between the two lower lamps was 0.9 m. They were situated 0.98 m beneath the shape. The upper lamp was situated 0.62 m above the shape.

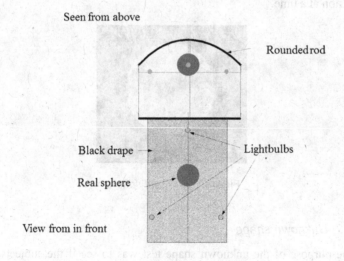

Figure 7.1. *Diagram of real equipment*

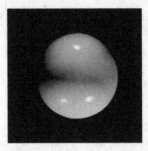

Figure 7.2. *Real sphere*

7.1.2.1.2. The virtual spheres

The standard sphere was thus a relatively accurate reproduction of the balloon (assumed spherical). It was green and also placed in front of a black background (Figure 7.3). We altered it dimension by dimension by less than 3% of the initial diameter (6mm) centered on the original value for the horizontal and vertical dimensions (called the width and the height, for ease of use further on) and by less than 12% of the initial diameter (24 mm) for variations in depth. These steps were specified in preliminary tests, carried out on three people. When one dimension was changed from the size of the original sphere, the others kept their original value, so as to change only one dimension at a time.

Figure 7.3. *Virtual sphere*

7.1.2.2. *Unknown shape*

The purpose of the unknown shape test was to see if the subjects were influenced by the sphere being a simple shape. It would be interesting to know the reaction of subjects faced with a totally unknown shape, whose radius of curvature is not fixed. This is a very interesting case because it is much closer to the shapes encountered in everyday life, especially in the automotive industry. However, the results were equally more complex to analyze.

7.1.2.2.1. The real shape

This unknown shape was a "deformed" sphere. It had the same average dimensions as the sphere in the previous section, but showed no symmetry (Figure 7.4). It was conceived and drawn using CATIA (CAD software) and constructed by rapid prototyping in rigid polystyrene foam with the help of Charly Robot, a digital machine tool. This shape was painted with the same green paint used for the real sphere and was held in the same position as the virtual form by three cables to avoid rotation.

It was also placed in front of a black backdrop (the same as for the sphere) and the same lighting was used (set up in the same way). In Figure 7.5, we see the overall set-up. Note that, in the photo, the lamps are obvious. During the tests, they were hidden (the one above by a drape, the one below by a board painted black).

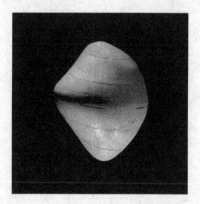

Figure 7.4. *Real unknown shape close-up*

7.1.2.2.2. The virtual shape

The basic virtual set-up was the same used for the design of the real set-up (using CATIA): green, and placed in front of a black backdrop (Figure 7.6).

Figure 7.5. *Complete real set-up, distance view*

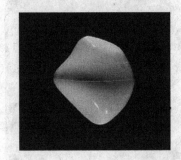

Figure 7.6. *Virtual unknown shape*

7.1.2.2.3. Experiments carried out

Sequences

We varied several parameters:

– distance between the two virtual cameras;

- the distance between the two virtual cameras is nil (monoscopic vision),

- the distance between the two virtual cameras is adjusted to the inter-pupillary distance of the subject,

- the distance between the two virtual cameras is double the inter-pupillary distance of the subject. This spacing was chosen so as to have the same deformation for each subject, whatever the distance between their eyes;

– tracking the subject's point of view;

- the subject is fixed in place and not allowed to move. The virtual camera is fixed in the direction of the area where the subject's head is sensed to be,

- the subject can move around and the virtual camera follows the position and orientation of the head;

– position of the shape with respect to the screen;

- the shape is on the screen, minimizing horizontal parallax,

- the shape is in front of the screen, which allows the subject to move more around it and reduces pixellation,

- the shape is behind the screen;

– the shape itself;

- the shape is a sphere, a basic shape well known to all subjects,

- the shape is at first unknown to the subjects.

We tested all the combinations of these parameters, giving us 36 combinations. When the point of view of the subject was not tracked, it therefore had a fixed position in both real and virtual worlds. This depended on the position of the virtual object. We defined these so that the subject was always 1.2 m away from the virtual as well as the real shape. This distance was chosen based on Johnston's results (see section 7.4.2.1) and based on the set-up of our equipment. The crosses on the ground defining these positions were shown to the subject before beginning the very first sequence, as shown in Figure 7.7.

When the shape is behind the screen and when the subject is fixed, the projection of the standard shape is 14 cm in diameter, corresponding to 87 pixels. Thus, a variation of 3% in its diameter changes 2.61 pixels. When the standard object is on the screen, however, its projection is 20 cm in diameter, thus 124 pixels. A 3% change in its diameter thus changes 3.72 pixels. Finally, when the standard shape is located in front of the screen, its projection measures 34 cm, or 211 pixels. A change in 3% adds or removes 6.33 pixels.

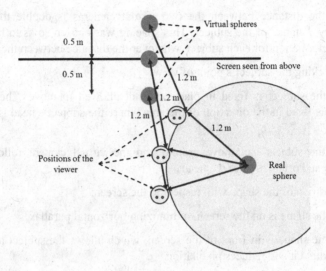

Figure 7.7. *Positioning of virtual and real objects and of the observer when the virtual object moves*

During a sequence

At the beginning of each sequence, instructions are given to the subject at the top left of the screen. The instructions may be:

> "*You can move around the room*"

or

> "*Stand on the cross which is nearest the screen*"

At the middle of the screen, a phrase invites the tester to press the "A" button on the WiiMote (the big round button on the front) as soon as they have read the instructions.

> "*Press A to begin*"

When a sequence begins, we begin varying the width of the virtual sphere. The subject is alerted all through the test by the phrase:

> "*The width of the sphere will vary. Is the virtual shape less wide (–) or wider (+)?*"

The subject is thus asked to press the "–" or "+" button of the controller (Figure 7.8) to give their opinion. When a button is pushed, a confirmation request appears on the screen:

"You pressed "–/+"; please press "A" to confirm"

Figure 7.8. *Screen capture during the test: requesting confirmation of a response*

When they validate their response, the object disappears for half a second to prevent comparison between the virtual shapes, before displaying the next variation. If the subject presses "A" without having given a response, the program does not validate and displays the same object again.

There are three series of seven random variations of the object's width, without replacement. After these 21 questions are posed, the subject is advised of the change in the dimension studied by the phrase:

"Change in dimension: the height will vary"

A new series of 21 questions on the height follows, and another on the depth. Each time the question changes:

"The height of the sphere will vary: is the virtual sphere smaller (–) or larger (+)?"

"The depth of the sphere will vary: is the virtual sphere less deep (–) or deeper (+)?"

During the tests with the unknown shape, obviously the word "sphere" in the previous questions is replaced by the word "shape".

7.1.2.3. *Result*

We therefore tested many conditions, but for our purposes, we only compared some of them. If you are curious and wish to know what results all the conditions gave, I invite you to read my thesis.

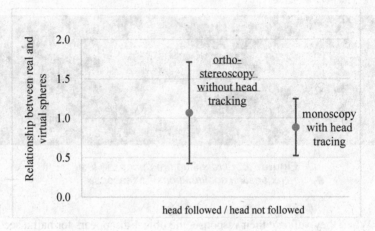

Figure 7.9. *Influence of stereoscopic disparities or motion parallax on the cumulative perception of the sphere and the random form*

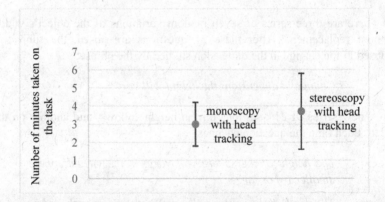

Figure 7.10. *Average time taken for the task*

7.1.2.3.1. Motion parallax or stereoscopy?

We show in Figure 7.9 the different influences of the two cues of depth perception: stereoscopy and motion parallax. The dots in the graph represent the point of subjective equalization (PSE), that is the diameter of the virtual object divided by that of the real object. The closer it is to 1, the better it is. The bars represent the just noticeable difference (JND) – the smaller it is, the better it is. We can see that motion parallax is a more effective cue for perception of curves than stereoscopic vision, allowing a more precise perception of curves.

We might think that the subject would take more time to perceive changes in shape when their point of view is tracked, since they are moving around the object. However, making the decision took longer when the point of view was not tracked than the time taken to move to another point of view when the latter was tracked. As shown in Figure 7.10, the average time taken for the task when the point of view was tracked in monoscopic vision was less than in stereoscopic vision with a tracked point of view. This difference is significant (probability of significance: 99%). Thus, it is preferable to be in monoscopic vision with a tracked point of view than in stereoscopic vision with point of view untracked, if we wish to minimize the time taken on a task.

7.1.2.3.2. Contribution of stereoscopy in the presence of motion parallax

We see in Figure 7.11 that there is improved accuracy in perception of curves (the length of the bar) when motion parallax is present. Stereoscopy is thus interesting, even when there is another depth cue.

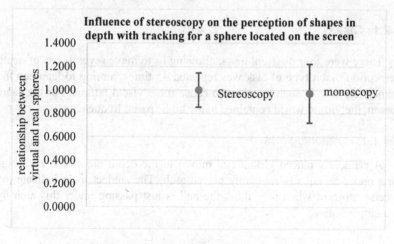

Figure 7.11. *Influence of stereoscopy on perception of curves when motion parallax is present*

7.1.3. *Hypothesis*

We thus present the hypothesis that stereoscopy is useful for carrying out tasks in a virtual world, but that it can also be temporarily interrupted without people noticing, so as to rest their visual system. We will also try to determine when it is preferable to activate stereoscopy, with respect to the type of task requested.

7.2. Experiment

The experiment therefore consists of presenting a subject with stimuli:

– in stereoscopy;

– in monoscopy;

– in intermittent stereoscopy, with stereoscopy in effect at the beginning or at the end of the task;

– to verify if visual fatigue is less in intermittent stereoscopy than in classical stereoscopy. At the same time, the tasks to be performed by the subject will give clues to the changes in depth perception induced by this change in projection.

This experiment was performed during the second-year Master's research of Ari Bouaniche under my supervision [BOU 15].

7.2.1. *Tasks*

There were four different tasks, allowing us to make several tests of depth perception. Each type of task was repeated 45 times, aiming to lengthen the immersion time in such a way as to cause some visual fatigue. For the same reason, the virtual world contained many high spatial frequencies.

7.2.1.1. *Positioning task*

A randomly placed virtual ball moves in the depth dimension and must pass under an equally randomly placed arch. The subject must indicate the precise moment when they think the ball is just passing under this arch by pressing a button.

7.2.1.2. Depth perception task

Spheres and cubes are placed at random depths, but at the same height and in a row facing the subject. The latter must indicate by pointing which sphere they think is closest to them.

7.2.1.3. Curve perception task

This task resembles that presented in section 7.1.1.1 and consists of indicating whether a cylinder which is deformed in the depth dimension has a circular base is flatter or more convex. Its position in space is chosen in a random manner, but its axis is always vertical.

7.2.1.4. Collision detection task

Two cubes are randomly placed, one on the left and one on the right side of the screen. They will move toward a random point on the opposite wall. After a certain time, the two cubes disappear. The subject must say if the two cubes would have collided had they not disappeared.

7.2.2. Experimental conditions

There are four experimental conditions corresponding to four projection situations. All these projection situations involve following the head, always allowing motion parallax.

7.2.2.1. Monoscopy

This is one of the two control conditions, which allow us to verify if the others have any effect with respect to a known situation. In this condition, the images of the left and the right eye are identical. However, the subject still wears stereoscopy glasses so that they are not aware that no stereoscopic depth is being projected.

7.2.2.2. Stereoscopy

In this other control condition, the stereoscopic images are calculated with an interocular distance corresponding to that of the subject.

7.2.2.3. Stereoscopy at the beginning

The two following conditions are those whose effects we will study. They both move from one control condition to the other. This condition presents a stereoscopic stimulus at the beginning of the task, immediately beginning to move the two virtual cameras closer together until we obtain a monoscopic stimulus. This movement lasts 3 sec.

7.2.2.4. Stereoscopy at the end

This is the inverse condition to the preceding. We begin by presenting a monoscopic stimulus, then after 4 sec, stereoscopy increases over 3 sec to stabilize at a stereoscopic stimulus adapted to the subject's interocular distance.

7.2.3. Subjects

These experiments were carried out on an inter-subjective basis. This means that a subject was only exposed to one of the four projection situations: monoscopic, stereoscopic, stereoscopic at the beginning and not at the end, and stereoscopic at the end and not at the beginning.

Sixty people undertook the experiment, or 15 per projection situation. Subjects of 40 years or over were excluded to avoid any presbyopia, whether detected or not, disrupting the measurement of ease of accommodation or punctum proximum of accommodation. Further, subjects presenting deficiencies at the level of stereoscopic vision were excluded from the protocol.

7.2.4. Measurements

7.2.4.1. Visual fatigue

Measurements of fatigue consisted of the same measurements as those explained in section 6.3.2.1, that is measurement of the punctum proximum of accommodation, ease of accommodation and stereoscopic acuity.

To these measurements we added other tests. The points of fusion and rupture were measured (see section 5.6). We presented two images (asterisks) with a disparity of 40 cm. Binocular status was also measured by requiring the subject to read words in monoscopy and in stereoscopy and in calculating the ratio of reading speeds.

7.2.4.2. *Perception*

Measurements of effectiveness were carried out for each task. For example:

– for the positioning task, the distance between the ball and the center of the arch is measured when the subject presses the button;

– in the depth perception task, the error in depth between the selected object and the nearest object is measured;

– in the curve perception task, the correct or incorrect answers given by the subject allow us to calculate the PSE as well as the threshold of discrimination;

– the collision detection task measures the error percentage in detection.

The time taken by the subjects to respond was measured for the collision detection task, the curve perception task and for the depth perception task.

7.3. Results

7.3.1. *Results for fatigue*

The measurements of differences in performance of the visual system were unfortunately not statistically significant. However, they may give some indications that might be explored further in future experiments.

7.3.1.1. *Points of rupture and fusion*

We can see in Figure 7.12 that stereoscopy being introduced at the end seems to cause less stress on the visual system. We suppose this to be due to gradual habituation to the stimulus.

Data on the point of fusion could not unfortunately be used. In fact, many subjects were able to fusion stimuli at very large disparity, and thus could not indicate the moment when double vision ceased because it was never present.

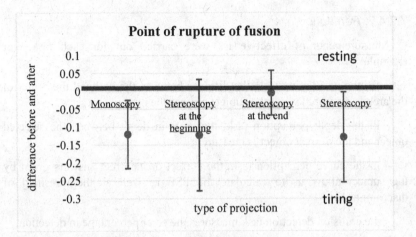

Figure 7.12. *Difference between points of rupture before and after experiment*

7.3.1.2. *Stereoscopic acuity*

In Figure 7.13, we can see that intermittent stereoscopy seems less stressful for the visual system. However, we cannot explain why the monoscopic condition received such a low score.

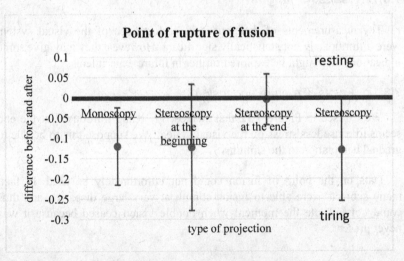

Figure 7.13. *Difference in stereoscopic acuity before and after experiment*

7.3.1.3. *Punctum proximum of accommodation*

In Figure 7.14, we can see that stereoscopy being introduced at the end seems to relieve the visual system. This would seem to correspond to the fact that the stereoscopic stimulus is progressively introduced to the visual system and is thus more easily accepted.

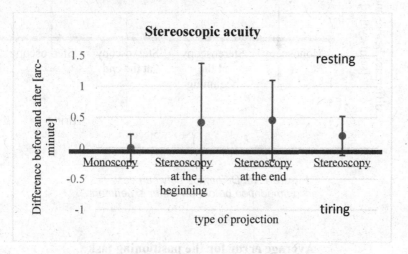

Figure 7.14. *Difference between the punctum proximum of accommodation before and after experiment*

7.3.1.4. *Ease of accommodation*

We see in Figure 7.15 that ease of accommodation was not greatly affected by our projections. On the other hand, we notice an anomaly in the values for stereoscopy.

7.3.2. *Perception results*

In the following figures:

– the points represent accuracy (calculated with the average), that is at what point the average of the responses is close to the ideal;

– the bars represent the precision (calculated with the standard deviation), that is the spread of the responses.

All the results below showed statistically significant differences.

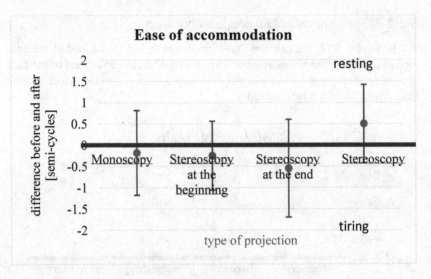

Figure 7.15. *Difference between ease of accommodation before and after experiment*

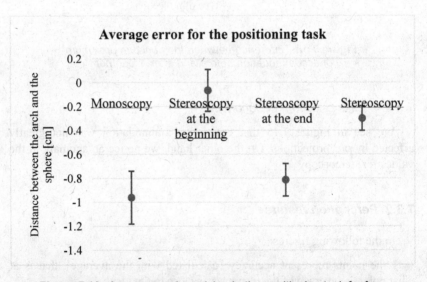

Figure 7.16. *Accuracy and precision in the positioning task for four conditions: monoscopic vision, stereoscopic vision, stereoscopic vision at the beginning but not at the end and stereoscopic vision at the end of the experiment*

7.3.2.1. *Positioning task*

In Figure 7.16, we see that the precision for stereoscopic vision at the beginning is very close to completely stereoscopic vision, even if most responses were given after stereoscopy had ceased. As for the accuracy of responses with stereoscopy at the end, it is close to monoscopic vision. It would seem then that for this type of task, the brain creates its map of depth very early and sticks to it. It is thus better for a positioning task to have stereoscopy at the beginning and remove it later.

7.3.2.2. *Depth perception task*

We can see in Figure 7.17 that the precision of the two intermittent conditions falls between the precisions for the monoscopic and stereoscopic conditions. The situation with stereoscopy at the beginning is nonetheless much closer to that for complete stereoscopic vision, while stereoscopy at the end is closer to that for monoscopic vision.

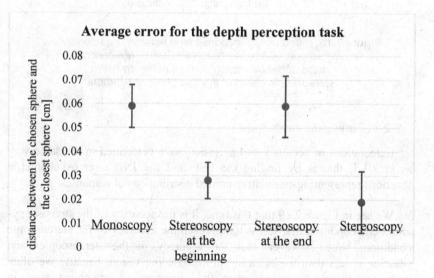

Figure 7.17. *Accuracy and position in the depth perception task for four conditions: monoscopic vision, stereoscopic vision, stereoscopic vision at the beginning and not at the end, and stereoscopic vision at the end of the experiment*

This distribution is seen in the time which the subjects took to respond, as shown in Figure 7.18.

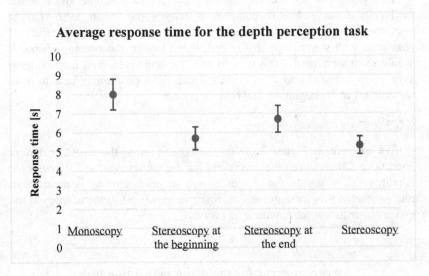

Figure 7.18. *Difference in response time between four conditions: monoscopic vision, stereoscopic vision, stereoscopic vision at the beginning and not at the end, and stereoscopic vision at the end of the experiment*

7.3.2.3. *Curve perception task*

Calculations of accuracy and precision were performed in the same way as in 7.1.1, that is by finding the PSE and the JND over psychometric functions representing cumulative normal distributions of responses.

We see in Figure 7.19 that this time, it is the accuracy of the stereoscopy-at-the-end condition that seems to approach the accuracy of the stereoscopic condition. Note, however, that the accuracy of the stereoscopicvision situation is less than the accuracy in monoscopic vision, because we often have a tendency to overestimate the curvature of an object seen in stereoscopy. In contrast, precision in stereoscopic vision is better, just as that for stereoscopy at the end is better. To put it another way, our vision is slightly deformed, but always in the same way, which helps with perceptive correction added by computer; it is enough to flatten our digital cylinder slightly for it to be seen as "circular".

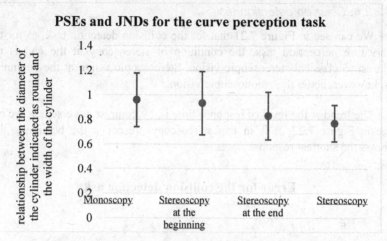

Figure 7.19. *Accuracy and precision in the curve perception task for four conditions: monoscopic vision, stereoscopic vision, stereoscopic vision at the beginning and not at the end, and stereoscopic vision at the endof the experiment*

We can see in Figure 7.20 that response times follow the same trend: for this task, it is stereoscopy at the end that is closer to the classical stereoscopic condition.

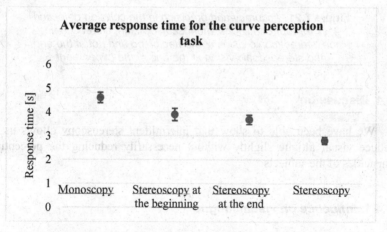

Figure 7.20. *Difference in time for the curve perception task for four conditions: monoscopic vision, stereoscopic vision, stereoscopic vision at the beginning and not at the end, and stereoscopic vision at the end of the experiment*

7.3.2.4. *Collision detection task*

We can see in Figure 7.21 that for the collision detection task, as for the curvature perception task, the condition of stereoscopy at the end is the closest to classical stereoscopic vision. Stereoscopic vision at the beginning is, however, better than monoscopic vision.

The trend at the level of response time is, by contrast, reversed, as we can see in Figure 7.22. It is in fact stereoscopy present at the beginning that shows the shortest response times.

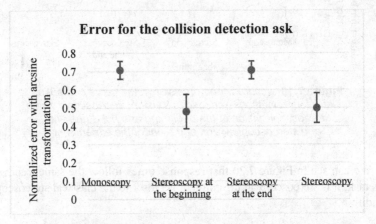

Figure 7.21. *Accuracy and precision in the collision detection task for four conditions: monoscopic vision, stereoscopic vision, stereoscopic vision at the beginning and not at the end, and stereoscopic vision at the end of the experiment*

7.4. Discussion

We have been able to show that intermittent stereoscopy allows us to reduce visual fatigue slightly without necessarily reducing the perceptive capacities of the subjects.

7.4.1. *Influence on visual fatigue*

We have shown that there is a tendency for visual fatigue to decrease, but that this decrease is not straightforward. It is shown especially in the fusional capacity of subjects as well as in stereoscopic acuity. Thus, it is stereoscopic capabilities that are better preserved with intermittent stereoscopy and particularly with stereoscopy at the end. This is in accordance with Neveu's work, which showed that the visual system undergoes fewer changes when the stereoscopic stimulus gradually appears [NEV 12].

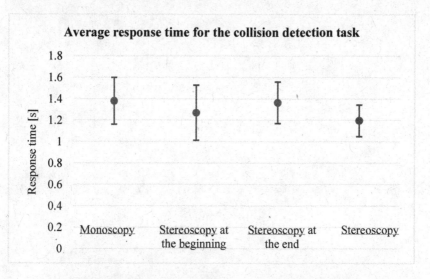

Figure 7.22. *Difference in time for the collision detection task for four conditions: monoscopic vision, stereoscopic vision, stereoscopic vision at the beginning and not at the end, and stereoscopic vision at the end of the experiment*

7.4.2. *Influence on visual perception*

The influence of intermittent stereoscopy on visual perception is more complex, as it seems to depend on the complexity of the task to be performed by the subject. For simple tasks like the first two, stereoscopy at the beginning seems to show a better record of improvement. In contrast, when the task is more complex, as for the curvature perception task that requires the visual system to calculate a second derivative (see section 4.4.2) or the collision detection task that requires following two objects in motion, it seems that stereoscopy at the end is more useful for solving the problem before the subject.

Conclusion

All through this work I have tried to explain why, in some cases, artificial stereoscopy can be stressful for the visual system. As with all technologies, it has its advantages and disadvantages and it is important to know all its ins and outs to draw the maximum benefit while minimizing the disadvantages. In fact, if we wish to use stereoscopy to best effect to improve depth perception, it is important to know its mechanisms as well as its implications in terms of oculomotor stresses to guarantee comfortable visualization for future users.

At the beginning of this book, I explained why and how stereoscopy is tiring for the visual system and what the short- and medium-term consequences of this fatigue might be. The second part of the book presents my research in trying to limit the conflicts caused by stereoscopy, particularly vergence-accommodation conflicts. Two major paths were explored:

– either we relax accommodation by creating blur, through suppressing high spatial frequencies;

– or we reduce the conflict by reducing vergence to arrive at a vergence point close to the accommodation point.

The first path is explored in Chapter 6, where we explain the algorithms for suppressing uncomfortable high spatial frequencies. This means those high frequencies situated in areas where the conflict is most marked, corresponding to the largest stereoscopic depths. We show the impact of this suppression on the subjects' oculomotor faculties to show that this kind of treatment can be put in place with beneficial effects.

The second path explored is that of the progressive suppression of depth. It is presented in Chapter 7. Since depth is not always present, it is important to show the effect on the oculomotor faculties of the subjects, but also on their perception in the presence of very simple tasks.

I hope that this book has enlightened you on the exciting technology that is stereoscopy, and that it will give you some idea of how to optimize the interfaces that you want to create; or, if you do not have an interface planned, it has interested you and given you at least as much pleasure as I got from writing it.

Bibliography

[ALB 02] ALBERT C., GOSSELIN L., Fatigue visuelle, document de référence, Direction de la santé publique, Paris, France, 2002.

[ALL 03] ALLISON R.S., ROGERS B.J., BRADSHAW M.F., "Geometric and induced effects in binocular stereopsis and motion parallax", *Vision Research*, vol. 43, nos. 1879–1893, 2003.

[AMZ 78] AMZALLAG F., PICCIOLLI N., BRY F., *Introduction à la statistique*, Herman, Paris, 1978.

[ARD 88] ARDEN G.B., "Le standard de mesure de l'acuité visuelle", *Journal Français d'Ophthalmologie*, vol. 11, no. 11, pp. 779–792, 1988.

[ASS 06] ASSOCIATION FRANÇAISE D'UROLOGIE, Utilisation de la robotique en chirurgie laparoscopique urologique: état de l'art, available at: http://urofrance.org/science-et-recherche/base-bibliographique/article/html/utilisation-de-la-robotique-en-chirurgie-laparoscopique-urologique-etat-de-lart.html, 2006.

[BAJ 76] BAJERY R., LEABERMAN L., "Texture gradient as depth cue", *SGIP*, vol. 5. pp. 52–67, 1976.

[BAN 12] BANDO T., IIJIMA A., YANO S., "Visual fatigue caused by stereoscopic images and the search for the requirement to prevent them: A review", *Displays, Assessing Comfortable 3D Visual Environment Based On Human Factors*, vol. 33, pp. 76–83, 2012.

[BAN 00] BANGOR A.W., *Display Technology and Ambient Illumination Influences on Visual Fatigue at VDT Workstations*, Virgina Institute and State University, Blacksburg, V.A., 2000.

[BAY 06] BAY H., TUYTELAARS T., VAN GOOL L., "SURF: speeded up robust features", *Computer Vision and Image Understanding*, vol. 110, no. 3, pp. 346–359, 2006.

[BEN 07] BENJAMIN W.J., *Borish's Clinical Refraction*, 2nd ed., Elsevier, Birmingham, 2007.

[BEN 16] BENOIT C., DUSSON A., Tipe sur la compression de données informatiques, available at: http://mp01.free.fr/comp/comp.htm, 2016.

[BER 96] BERGHOLM F., FRANCISCO A., "On the horopter and Hering-Hillebrand deviation", *IEEE Proceedings of Second Workshop on Cybernetic Vision*, Sao Carlos, Brazil, 1996.

[BON 86] BONNET C., *Manuel pratique de psychophysique*, Armand Colin, Paris, 1986.

[BOU 15] BOUANICHE A., Explorer la stéréoscopie intermittente: Son influence sur la perception et la fatigue visuelle, Thesis, University of Paris 8, 2015.

[BOY 00] BOYER J., *Méthodes statistiques: médecine-biologie*, Estem, Paris, 2000.

[BRA 99] BRADSHAW M.F., ROGERS B.J., "Sensitivity to horizontal and vertical corrugations defined by binocular disparity", *Vision Research*, vol. 39, pp. 3049–3056, 1999.

[BUT 88] BUTTS D.R., MCALLISTER D.F., "Implementation of true 3-D cursors in computer graphics", *Three-Dimensional Imaging and Remote Sensing Imaging*, vol. 902, pp. 74–83, 1988.

[CAG 93] CAGENELLO R., ROGERS B.J., "Anisotropy in perception of stereoscopic surfaces: the role of orientation disparity", *Vision Research*, vol. 33, pp. 2189–2201, 1993.

[CAH 90] CAHEN O., *L'image en relief: de la photographie stéréoscopique à la vidéo 3D*, Masson, Paris, 1990.

[CAM 68] CAMPBELL F., ROBSON J., "Application of Fourier analysis to the visibility of gratings", *Journal of Physiology*, pp. 551–566, 1968.

[COS 96] COSTELLO P.J., HOWARTH P.A., The visual effects of immersion in four virtual environments, Research Report VISERG, Sophia Antipolis, France, 1996.

[DAG 98] DAGNELIE P., *Statistique théorique et appliquée: inférence statistique à une et à deux dimensions*, De Boek University, Brussels, Belgium, 1998.

[DEV 88] DEVALOIS R., DEVALOIS K., *Spatial Vision*, Oxford University Press, 1988.

[DEV 08] DEVISME C., Etude de l'influence des disparités horizontales et verticales sur la perception de la profondeur en champ visuel périphérique, PhD Thesis, Univeristy of Paris 6, 2008.

[DRO 92] DROESBEKE J.-J. *Elements de statistique*, Edition de l'université libre de Bruxelles, 1992.

[DUR 95] DURGIN F.H., PROFFITT D.R., OLSON T. J. *et al.*, "Comparing depth from binocular disparity to depth from motion", *Journal of Experimental Psychology, Human Perception and Performance*, vol. 21, no. 3, pp. 679–699, 1995.

[EGG 96] EGGLESTON R.G., JANSON W.P., ALDRICH K.A., "Virtual reality system effects on size-distance judgments in a virtual environment", *Proceedings of the IEEE Virtual Reality*, 1996.

[ESP 08] ESPINASSE-BERROD M.-A., PÉCHEREAU A. *Strabologie: Approches diagnostique et thérapeutique*, Elsevier Masson, Paris, 2008.

[FEC 60] FECHNER G.T., *Eléments de psychophysique*, Breitkopf and Härtel, Leipzig, 1860.

[FEN 67] FENDER D., JULESZ B., "Extension of panum's area", *The Optical Society of America*, vol. 57, pp. 819–830, 1967.

[FOR 11] FORTUIN M.F., LAMBOOIJ M.T., IJSSELSTEIJN W.A. *et al.*, "An exploration of the initial effects of stereoscopic displays on optometric parameters", vol. 31, pp. 33–44, 2011.

[FUC 06] FUCHS P., *La restitution visuelle stéréoscopique – traité de la réalité virtutelle*, Presses de l'Ecole des mines de Paris, 2006.

[FUC 95] FUCHS P., ERNADOTTE D., MAMAN D. *et al.*, "Téléprésence virtuelle stéréoscopique", *Interface des Mondes Réels et Virtuels*, pp. 77–91, 1995.

[FUC 03] FUCHS P., PAPIN J.-P., *Le sens et les réponses motrices de l'homme - traité de la réalité virtuelle*, Presses de l'Ecole des mines de Paris, 2003.

[FUJ 14] FUJIKAKE K., OMORI M., HASEGAWA S. *et al.*, "Stereoscopic displays and accommodative focus", *Forma*, vol. 29, pp. S53-S63, 2014.

[GAB 46] GABOR D., "Theory of communication", *Journal of IEEE*, vol. 93, no. 3, pp. 429–457,1946.

[GIB 50] GIBSON J. J., *The Perception of the Visual Word*, Houghton Mifflin, Boston, 1950.

[GIL 98] GILLAM B., CHAMBERS D., LAWERGREN B., "Postfusional latency in stereoscopic slant perception and the primitives of stereopsis", *Journal of Experimental Psychology: Human Perception and Performance*, vol. 14, pp. 163–176,1988.

[GIL 83] GILLAM B., LAWERGREN B., "The induced effect vertical disparity and steroscopic theory", *Perception and Psychophysics*, vol. 34, pp. 121–130, 1983.

[GLE 94] GLENNERSTER A., ROGER S.J.B., BRADSHAW M.F., "The effect of (i) differents cues and (ii) the observer's task in stereoscopic depth constancy", *Investigative Ophthalmology and Visual Science*, vol. 145, pp. 159–161, 1994.

[GOL 03] GOLDSTEIN E.B., *Sensation and Perception*, Wadsworth Publishing Company, 2003.

[GOW 89] GOWER D.W., FOWLKES J.E., Simulator Sickness in the UH-60 (Black Hawk) Flight Simulator, available at: http://www.usaarl.army.mil/TechReports/89-25.pdf, 1989.

[GRE 03] GRENEZ F., *Théorie des signaux*, Presse universitaire de Bruxelles, 2003.

[GUI 79] GUILLAUME P. *La psychologie de la forme*, Flammarion, Paris, 1979.

[HEC 89] HECKMANN T., SCHOR C.M., "Panum's fusional area estimated with a criterion-free technique", *Perception and Psychophysics*, vol. 45, pp. 297–306, 1989.

[HIL 08] HILLAIRE S., LECUYER A., COZOT R., "Using an eye-tracking system to improve depth-of-field blur effect and camera motion in virtual environments", *Proceedings of IEEE Virtual Reality*, pp. 47–51, 2008.

[HIL 07] HILLAIRE S., LECUYER A., COZOT R. *et al.*, "Depth of field blur effects for first person navigation in virtual environments", *Proceedings of ACM Symposium on Virtual Reality Software and Technology*, pp. 204–207, 2007.

[HOF 08] HOFFMAN D.M., GIRSHICK A.R., AKELEY K., "Vergence–accommodation conflicts hinder visual performance and cause visual fatigue", *Journal of Visualization*, vol. 8, no. 33, 2008.

[HOL 41] HOLWAY A.H., BORING E.G., "Determinants of apparent visual size with distance variant", *American Journal of Psychology*, vol. 54, no. 1, pp. 21–37, 1941.

[HOW 95] HOWARD I. P., ROGERS B.J., *Binocular Vision and Stereopsis*, Oxford University Press, 1995.

[HOW 99] HOWARTH P.A., "Oculomotor changes within virtual environments", *Applied Ergonomics*, vol. 30, pp. 59–67, 1999.

[HUB 95] HUBBARD B.B., *Ondes et ondelettes la saga d'un outil mathématique*, Belin pour la science, Paris, 1995.

[HUG 65] HUGONNIER S., HUGONNIER R., *Strabismes, hétérophories, paralysie oculo-motrices: les déséquilibres oculo-moteurs en clinique*, Masson et Cie Saint-Ouen, Maillet, 1965.

[JOH 91] JOHNSTON E.B., "Systematic distortions of shape from stereopsis", *Vision Research*, vol. 31, pp. 1351–1360, 1991.

[JON 01] JONES G., LEE D., HOLLIMAN N. *et al.*, "Controlling perceived depth in stereoscopic image", *Proceedings of IEEE*, vol. 4297, pp. 42–53, 2001.

[JUL 71] JULESZ B., *Foundations of Cyclopean Perception*, University of Chicago Press, 1971.

[KAR 13] KARPICKA E., HOWARTH P.A., "Heterophoria adaptation during the viewing of 3D stereoscopic stimuli", *Ophthalmic Physiol Opt*, vol. 33, pp. 604–610, 2013.

[KEL 80] KELLOG R. S., CASTORE C., COWARD R., "Psychophysiological effects of training in a full vision simulator", *Annual Scientific Meeting of the Aerospace Medical Association*, 1980.

[KIM 11] KIM D., CHOI S., PARK S. *et al.*, "Stereoscopic visual fatigue measurement based on fusional response curve and eye-blinks", *17th International Conference on Digital Signal Processing*, 2011.

[KOE 96] KOENDERINK J.J., VAN DOORN A.J., KOPPERS A.M.L., "Pictorial surface attitude and local depth comparisons", *Perception and Psychophysics*, vol. 58, no. 2, pp. 162–17, 1996.

[KOE 92] KOENDERINK J.J., VAN DOORN A.J., KOPPERS A.M.L., "Surface perception in picture", *Perception and Psychophysics*, vol. 52, no. 5, pp. 482–496, 1992.

[KOO 01] KOOI F.L., TOET A., "Visual comfort of binocular and 3D displays", *Proceedings of SPIE*, vol. 4299, pp. 586–592, 2001.

[LAM 09] LAMBOOIJ M., FORTUIN M., HEYNDERICKX I. *et al.*, "Visual discomfort and visual fatigue of stereoscopic displays: a review", *Journal of Imaging Science and Technology*, vol. 53, p. 30201–1–30201–14, 2009.

[LAM 09] LAMBOOIJ M., FORTUIN M., IJSEELSETIN W. *et al* , "Measuring visual discomfort associated with 3D dispalys", *Proceedings of SPIE*, vol. 7237, 2009.

[LAM 11] LAMBOOIJ M., FORTUIN M., IJSSELSTEIJN W.A. et al., "Susceptibility to visual discomfort of 3D displays by visual performance measures", *IEEE Transactions on Circuits and Systems for Video Technology*, vol. 21, pp. 1913–1923, 2011.

[LAV 00] LAVIOLA J.J., "A discussion of cybersickness in virtual environments", *SIGCHI Bulletin*, vol. 32, no. 1, pp. 47–56, 2000.

[LEM 06] LEMAIRE P., *Abrégé de psychophysique cognitive*, De Boeck, Paris, 2006.

[LER 09] LEROY L., Interfaçage visual stéréoscopique: diminution de la fatigue visuelle et caractérisation de la perception des formes, Thesis, École Nationale Supérieure des Mines de Paris, 2009.

[LEV 65] LEVELT W.J.M., On Binocular Rivalry, Institute for Perception, Soesterberg, 1965.

[LEV 66] LEVELT W.J.M., "The alternation process in binocular rivalry", *British Journal Psychology*, vol. 58, pp. 143–145, 1966.

[LUO 07] LUO X., KENYON R., KAMPER D. *et al.*, "The effect of scene complexity, stereovision, and motion parallax on size constancy in virtual environment", *IEEE Virtual Reality*, 2007.

[MAC 93] MACKENZIE I.S., WARE C., "Lag as a determinant of human performance in interactive systems", *Proceedings of the ACM Conference on Human Factors in Computing System*, pp. 488–493, 1993.

[MAL 00] MALLAT S., *Une exporation des signaux en ondelettes*. Éditions de l'École Polytechnique, Paris. 2000.

[MAN 02] MANAN F.A., JENKINS T.C.A., COLLINGE A.J., "The effect of clinical visual stress on stereoacuity measured with the TNO test", *Malaysian Journal of Medical Sciences*, vol. 8, pp. 25–31, 2002.

[MAR 82] MARR D., *Vision: a Computational Investigation into the Human Representation and Processing of Visual Information*, Freeman, New York, 1982.

[MAS 06] MASSOT C., Texture et perception 3D dans les scènes naturelles: modèles d'inspiration, PhD Thesis, University Joseph Fourier de Grenoble, 2006.

[MC2 16] MC2 MEDICAL, Test du TNO, available at: http://mc2medical.com/index.php?page=orthoptie&cat=test-vision-stereoscopie& fiche=test-tno, 2016.

[MCK 93] MCKEE S.P., "The spatial requirements for fine stereoacuity", *Vision Research*, vol. 23, no. 191–198, 1993.

[MED 15]. MEDICAL VISION, http://www.medicalvision.it/english/stereoscopic-test.html, acccessed October 2015.

[MEY 92] MEYER I., *Les ondelettes algorithmes et applications*, Armand Colin, Paris 1992.

[MIT 66] MITCHELL D.E., "Retinal disparity and diplopia", *Vision Research*, vol. 6, pp. 441–451, 1966.

[MON 70] MONEY K.E., "Motion sickness", *Psychological Reviews*, vol. 50, no. 1, pp. 1–39, 1970.

[NAK 83] NAKAYAMA K., *Kinematics of Normal and Strabismic Eyes. In:* SCHOR C., CIUFFREDA K., *Vergence Eye Movements: Basics and Clinical Aspects*, Butterworth, London–Boston, 1983.

[NEV 12] NEVEU P., L'impact des dispositifs de visualization en relief sur les composantes oculomotrices d'accommodation et de vergence, Thesis, Paris, 2012.

[NEV 08] NEVEU P., Retentissement du sur-écartement inter-pupillaire sur l'équilibre oculomoteur, Masters Thesis, 2008.

[NEV 10] NEVEU P., PRIOT A.-E., PLANTIER J., "Short exposure to telestereoscope affects the oculomotor system", *Ophthalmic Physiol Opt*, vol. 30, pp. 806–815, 2010.

[NIE 84] NIELSEN K.R.K., POGGIO T., "Vertical image registration in stereopsis v.", *Vision Research*, vol. 24, pp. 1133–1140, 1984.

[NOR 84] NORCIA A.M., TYLER C.W., "Temporal frequency limits for stereoscopic apparent motion processes", *Vision Research*, vol. 24, pp. 395–401, 1984.

[OGL 50] OGLE K.N., *Research in Binocular Vision*, W.B. Saunders Compagny, Philadelphia–London, 1950.

[OLI 06] OLIVIA, A., TORRALBA A., SCHYNS P. G., "Hybridimage", *ACM Transaction on Graphics*, vol. 25, no. 3, pp. 527–530, 2006.

[ØST 35] ØSTERBERG G., "Topography of the layer of rods and cones in the human retina", *Acta Ophthalmologica*, vol. 6, pp.1–102, 1935.

[PAL 04] PALJIC A., Interaction en environnements immersifs et retours d'effort passif, Thesis, University of Paris 6, 2004.

[PAL 02] PALJIC A., COQUILLART S., BURKHARDT J.-M., "A study of distance of manipulation on the responsive workbench", *Immersive Projection Technology Symposium*, 2002.

[PAL 61] PALMER D.A., "Measurement of the horizontal extent of Panum's area by a method of constant stimuli", *Opical Acta*, vol. 8, pp. 151–159, 1961.

[PAL 99] PALMER S.E., *Vision Science: Photons to Phenomenology*, MIT Press, Oxford,1999.

[PER 98] PERRIN J., Profondeur et binocularité: algorithmie, étude psychophysique et intérêt pour l'ergonomie des interface stéréoscopiques, Thesis, Ecole des Mines de Paris, 1998.

[PHO 92] PHOTO FRIDAY, Photo Friday: Monitor Calibration Tool, available at www.photofriday.com/calibrate.php, accessed: 24 June 2009.

[PRE 09] PRECISION-VISION, available at: http: //precision-vision.com, accessed: June 2009.

[PRI 98] PRINCE S.J.D., ROGERS B.J., "Sensitivity to disparity corrugations in peripheral vision", *Vision Research*, vol. 38, pp. 2533–2537, 1998.

[RAM 96] RAMOUSSE R., LE BERRE M., LE GUELTE L., Introduction aux statistiques, available at: www.cons-dev.org/elearning/stat/, 1996.

[RAN 01] RANCHIN T., Analyse multirésolution et transformée en ondelettes, Thesis, Ecole des Mines de Paris, 2001.

[REA 15] READ J.C.A., SIMONOTTO J., BOHR I. *et al.*, "Balance and coordination after viewing stereoscopic 3D television", *Royal Society Open Science*, vol. 2, 2015.

[REA 75] REASON J.T., BRAND J.J., *Motion Sickness*, Academic Press, London, 1975.

[RIC 71] RICHARDS W., "Independence of Panum's near and far limits", *American Journal of Optometry*, vol. 48, pp. 103–109, 1971.

[ROG 83] ROGERS B.J., GRAHAM M.E., "Anisotropies in the perception of three-dimensional surfaces", *Science*, vol. 221, pp. 1409–1411, 1983.

[ROG 89] ROGERS B., CAGENELLO R., "Disparity curvature and the perception of three-dimensional surfaces", *Nature*, vol. 339, pp. 261–270, 1989.

[ROU 95] ROUMES C., Contenu fréquentiel de l'image et vision binoculaire – Etude psychophysique chez l'homme, Thesis, University of Paris, 1995.

[ROU 92] ROUMES C., PLANTIER J., MENU J.-P., "Local contrast: a quantification tool for stereo-image", *Proceedings of IEEE*, vol. 5, pp. 2098–2099, 1992.

[RUS 99] RUSHTON S.K., MC RIDDELL P., "Developing visual system and exposure to virtual reality and stereo display: some concerns and speculation about the demands on accomodation and vergence", *Applied Ergonomics*, vol. 30, pp. 69–78, 1999.

[SAK 95] SAKAI K., FINKEL H., "Characterisation of spatial frequency in the perception of shape form texture", *Journal of the Optical Society of America A*, no. 12, pp. 1208–1224, 1995.

[SCA 06] SCARFE P., HIBBARD P., "Disparity-defined objects moving in depth do not elicit three-dimensional shape constancy", *Vision Research*, vol. 46, no. 10, pp. 1599–1610, 2006.

[SCH 86] SCHOR C.M., "Adaptive regulation of accommodative vergence and vergence accommodation", *American Journal of Optometry and Physiological Optics*, vol. 65, pp. 168–173, 1986.

[SCH 89] SCHOR C.M., HECKMANN T., TYLE C.W., "Binocular fusion limits are independant of contrast, luminance gradient and component phases", *Vision Research*, vol. 29, pp. 821–835,1989.

[SCH 86] SCHOR C.M., ROBERSTON K.M., WESSON M., "Binocular sensory vision is limited by spatial resolution", *Vision Research*, vol. 24, pp. 573–578,1986.

[SCH 81] SCHOR C.M., TYLER C.W., "Spatio temporal properties of Panum's fusional area", *Vision Research*, vol. 21, pp. 683–692,1981.

[SHE 03] SHEEDY J.E., HAYES J.N., ENGLE J., "Is all asthenopia the same?", *Optom Vis Sci*, vol. 80, pp. 732–739, 2003.

[SHI 11] SHIBATA T., KIM J., HOFFMAN D.M. *et al.*, "The zone of comfort: Predicting visual discomfort with stereo displays", *Journal of Vision*, vol. 11, p. 11, 2011.

[STE 99] STELMACH L., TAM W.J., MEEGAN D., "Perceptual basis of stereoscopic video", *Proceedings of SPIE*, vol. 3639, pp. 260–265, 1999.

[STE 00] STELMACH L., TAM W.J., MEEGAN D. *et al.*, "Human perception of mismatched stereoscopic 3D inputs", *IEEE International Conference on Image Processing*, vol. 1, pp. 5–8, 2000.

[STE 79] STEVENS K.S., Surface perception from local analysis of texture and contour, PhD Thesis, MIT, 1979.

[TAM 98] TAM W.J., STELMACH L.B., CORRIVEAU P., "Psychovisual aspects of viewing stereoscopic video sequences", *Proceedings of SPIE*, vol. 3295, pp. 226–235, 1998.

[TIB 84] TIBERGHIEN G., *Initiation à la psychophysique*, Presses Univeritaires de France, Paris, 1984.

[TIG14] TIGUEMOUNINE K., Reéducation des yeux et de la tête: traitements des céphalées et des douleurs crânio-cervico-faciales, available at: http://www.sel-katia-tiguemounine-masseurs-kinesitherapeutes.fr/index.php/reeducation-posturale-globale-rpg/douleurs-tete-yeux-et-cervicales, 2014.

[TYR 90] TYRRELL R.A. *et al.*, "The relation of vergence effort to reports of visual fatigue following prolonged near work", *Human Factors*, vol. 32, pp. 341–357, 1990.

[UPV 09] UPVECTOR, http://www.upvector.com, accessed: June 20, 2009.

[VAL 62] VALYUS N., *Stereoscopy*, Focal Press, London, 1962.

[VIO 01] VIOLA P., JONES M., "Rapid object detection using boosted cascade of simple features", *IEEE Computer Society Conference on Computer Vision and Pattern Recognition*, vol. 1, pp. 5–11, 2001.

[WAN 95] WANN J.P., RUSHTON S., WILLIAMS M., "Natural problems for stereoscopic depth perception in virtual environments", *Vision Research*, vol. 35, no. 6, pp. 2731–2736, 1995.

[WAT 83] WATSON A., BARLOW H., ROBSON J., "What does the eye see the best?", *Nature*, vol. 302, pp. 419–422, 1983.

[WIL 79] WILSON H., BERGEN J., "A four mechanism model for spatial vision", *Vision Research*, pp. 19–32, 1979..

[WIL83]WILSON H., MCFARLANE D., PHILLIPS G., "Spatial frequency tuning of orientation selective units estimated by oblique masking", *Vision Research*, vol. 19, no. 9, pp. 873–882, 1983.

[WOO 74] WOO G.C.S., "The effect of exposure time on the foveal size of Panum's area", *Vision Research*, vol. 14, pp. 473–480, 1974.

[WOP 95] WOPKING M., "Viewing comfort with stereoscopic pixture: an experiment study on the subjective effects of disparity magnitude and depth of focus", *Journal of SID*, vol. 3, pp. 101–103, 1995.

[YAN 02] YANO S., IDE S., MITUHASHI T. *et al.*, "A study of visual fatigue and visual comfort for 3d hdtv/hdtv images", *Stereoscopic Displays*, vol. 213, pp. 191–201, 2002.

[YOU 06] YOUNG S.D., ADELSTEIN B.D., ELLIS S.R., "Demand characteristics of a questionnaire used to asses motion sickness in a virtual environment", *Proceedings of the IEEE Virtual Reality Conference*, pp. 97–102, 2006.

[ZEI 09] ZEISS, www.zeiss.com, accessed June 2009.

Index

Other titles from

in

Computer Engineering

2016

DEROUSSI Laurent
Metaheuristics for Logistics (Metaheuristics Set – Volume 4)

LABADIE Nacima, PRINS Christian, PRODHON Caroline
*Metaheuristics for Vehicle Routing Problems
(Metaheuristics Set – Volume 3)*

MAGOULÈS Frédéric, ZHAO Hai-Xiang
Data Mining and Machine Learning in Building Energy Analysis

2015

BARBIER Franck, RECOUSSINE Jean-Luc
*COBOL Software Modernization: From Principles to Implementation with
the BLU AGE® Method*

CHEN Ken
*Performance Evaluation by Simulation and Analysis with Applications to
Computer Networks*

CLERC Maurice
Guided Randomness in Optimization (Metaheuristics Set – Volume 1)

QUESNEL Flavien
Scheduling of Large-scale Virtualized Infrastructures: Toward Cooperative Management

RIGO Michel
Formal Languages, Automata and Numeration Systems 1: Introduction to Combinatorics on Words
Formal Languages, Automata and Numeration Systems 2: Applications to Recognizability and Decidability

SAINT-DIZIER Patrick
Musical Rhetoric: Foundations and Annotation Schemes

TOUATI Sid, DE DINECHIN Benoit
Advanced Backend Optimization

2013

ANDRÉ Etienne, SOULAT Romain
The Inverse Method: Parametric Verification of Real-time Embedded Systems

BOULANGER Jean-Louis
Safety Management for Software-based Equipment

DELAHAYE Daniel, PUECHMOREL Stéphane
Modeling and Optimization of Air Traffic

FRANCOPOULO Gil
LMF — Lexical Markup Framework

GHÉDIRA Khaled
Constraint Satisfaction Problems

ROCHANGE Christine, UHRIG Sascha, SAINRAT Pascal
Time-Predictable Architectures

WAHBI Mohamed
Algorithms and Ordering Heuristics for Distributed Constraint Satisfaction Problems

ZELM Martin *et al.*
Enterprise Interoperability

2012

ARBOLEDA Hugo, ROYER Jean-Claude
Model-Driven and Software Product Line Engineering

BLANCHET Gérard, DUPOUY Bertrand
Computer Architecture

BOULANGER Jean-Louis
Industrial Use of Formal Methods: Formal Verification

BOULANGER Jean-Louis
Formal Method: Industrial Use from Model to the Code

CALVARY Gaëlle, DELOT Thierry, SÈDES Florence, TIGLI Jean-Yves
Computer Science and Ambient Intelligence

MAHOUT Vincent
Assembly Language Programming: ARM Cortex-M3 2.0: Organization, Innovation and Territory

MARLET Renaud
Program Specialization

SOTO Maria, SEVAUX Marc, ROSSI André, LAURENT Johann
Memory Allocation Problems in Embedded Systems: Optimization Methods

2011

BICHOT Charles-Edmond, SIARRY Patrick
Graph Partitioning

BOULANGER Jean-Louis
Static Analysis of Software: The Abstract Interpretation

PASCHOS Vangelis Th
Combinatorial Optimization and Theoretical Computer Science: Interfaces and Perspectives

WALDNER Jean-Baptiste
Nanocomputers and Swarm Intelligence

2007

BENHAMOU Frédéric, JUSSIEN Narendra, O'SULLIVAN Barry
Trends in Constraint Programming

JUSSIEN Narendra
A to Z of Sudoku

2006

BABAU Jean-Philippe *et al.*
From MDD Concepts to Experiments and Illustrations – DRES 2006

HABRIAS Henri, FRAPPIER Marc
Software Specification Methods

MURAT Cecile, PASCHOS Vangelis Th
Probabilistic Combinatorial Optimization on Graphs

PANETTO Hervé, BOUDJLIDA Nacer
Interoperability for Enterprise Software and Applications 2006 / IFAC-IFIP I-ESA'2006

2005

GÉRARD Sébastien *et al.*
Model Driven Engineering for Distributed Real Time Embedded Systems

PANETTO Hervé
Interoperability of Enterprise Software and Applications 2005